with Liberty
and Justice for all.

In God we trust.

CHURCH!
IT'S TIME TO
RUMBLE

Dal Mize

NEWMAN SPRINGS PUBLISHING
320 Broad Street
Red Bank, NJ 07701

First originally published by Newman Springs Publishing 2022

Scripture quotations marked "NLT" are taken from the Holy Bible, New Living Translation, Copyright © 1996. Used by permission of the Tyn dale House Publication, Inc. All rights reserved.

ISBN 978-1-68498-016-1 (Paperback)
ISBN 978-1-68498-017-8 (Digital)

Printed in the United States of America

Sandy,
The Joy of the Lord is your
strength. God Blessings

Dal Mize

If my people, who are called by my name will humble themselves
and pray and seek my face and turn from their wicked ways, I will
hear from heaven and will forgive their sins and heal their land.

—2 Chr 7:14 (NLT)

PREFACE

A note from the author:

I felt I had to give you a background on why this book was written. After you read this preface, you should have a better idea why I chose to title the book *Church! It's Time to Rumble.*

> Shout with joy to the Lord, 0 earth! Worship the Lord with gladness. Come before Him, singing with joy. Acknowledge that the Lord is God! He made us, and we are His. We are His people, the sheep of His pasture. Enter His gates with thanksgiving; go into His courts with praise. Give thanks to Him and bless His HOLY NAME. (Psalm 100 NLT)

Wake up, America. Right at the time we need God, we seem to have retreated to our closets. Our nation, for many years, has been the leader and the strongest nation in the world, has become "a nation divided." Contrary to what it says in our pledge, it no longer seems to be one nation under God.

Never in the history of this nation, has our country been so divided. Our division is even greater than the division between the North and South was in the 1860s, which resulted in the great Civil War. That war proved to be one of the bloodiest wars in which this nation has ever been involved. It positioned families against families, brothers against brothers, fathers against sons and reversed love for each other into a hate for mankind. There is no doubt that this was, without question, the lowest point in America's history. Just as

President Lincoln said in his famous speech in Gettysburg, that war will be remembered in infamy.

Many would question that we are now more divided than our nation was during the great Civil War. It would seem, with all the new technology, that America would be more aware of what has been happening in our country.

Our constitution was written to ensure that when a person is elected to serve in the congress of the United States of America that he will pledge allegiance to one nation, under God, and he will also honor and serve the republic for which he has been elected. Somehow, through the years, there has developed a conflict between the church and state that has split our nation down the middle. It is hard to believe more than half of those serving in our government are trying to remove the "under God" clause from our pledge and are petitioning to convert our capitalist government to a socialist government.

There seems to be a great division taking place in America that has divided our country to a point that our government is split between the liberal and the conservative. It's hard to believe that this is happening to the greatest and most powerful nation on this planet. There is no doubt that we are in a war between the "we the people" and big government. But what makes our current split a bigger problem is that the war between church and state has grown so big that it has caused this division in our government. Believe me, it is a holy war. And if we don't get it under control, it will destroy the great America we once knew.

Our forefathers, from the time they first landed at Plymouth Rock, vowed to establish this country as a Christian nation that was conceived in liberty and founded on the principles of the Holy Bible. They installed a constitution that brought forth rules and regulations that were centered around the Christian belief. They stressed that this government would be a government of the people, by the people, and for the people. It would be a government that would operate under a capitalist form of government and would be founded as a democratic republic. In fact, there was great effort to build an esprit de corps of respect and honor for this republic and its flag by using and stressing the love of God as a theme. They even wrote and installed a national pledge that was taught to all their children and recited each day when they started school. They established churches and places where the people could go to worship Christ as their Savior.

Nowadays, many of our schools, because of the vast number of different nationalities and beliefs, no longer recite this pledge, and the freedom to offer prayers in school has been removed. It might bring a lot of unity to this nation if we reinstate this pledge and return prayer into our schools. It has always bothered me that when we opened our country to people of other nations, why we had to change our country's rules to accommodate immigrants from other countries. When I was a youngster just starting school, I was taught to stand with my hand over my heart and recite the Pledge of Allegiance. Then after the pledge, there was a general prayer given to ask God to be with us and direct us during that day. When I was inducted into the air force and in many of my training classes, we often started class with this pledge. This is no longer done because some of those from other nations complained that it violated the constitution of the United States. I am sure that many of those who immigrated to this country did not share the freedom of religion and respect for our nation, but they were quick to jump on the ship to become part of our society. Instead of adapting to our ways, which our forefathers established and to respect this country and beliefs, they pushed for us to change our ways to conform to their beliefs and their ways.

I remember when I was sent overseas to a different country, one of the things our commanders made sure we understood, "When in another country, we always must make sure that we conformed to that country's ways and actions of the country we were visiting."

Respect for others and our country seems to have faded from our country. For example, I have always wondered why, as a nation, we have not stressed that those who immigrate to our country at least conform to our laws. It seems that most immigrants, whom we have taken in as citizens of this great nation, seem to push for us to conform to their ways instead of them "blending" into our ways.

If they came to America to become an American citizen, why not teach them, upon arrival, to learn and recite the pledge: "I pledge allegiance to the flag of the United States of America, and to the republic for which it stands, one nation under God, indivisible with liberty and justice for all"? If they don't do that, then send them back to their country. They don't have to convert to our religious beliefs, but we would be within our rights to give them a Bible. But instead of that, we elect them to our congress and even allow them to wear their native dress.

I pray this book will give a better understanding how much of the greatness of the nation has been taken away because America has turned away from the principles and respect for each other and God. In addition, there has been a push to revert our nation to a socialist nation where usually one man is elevated to dictatorship of the government. He not only owns the country but owns the people.

If we choose to become a socialist country, there is no longer freedom to worship and trust in the God of our choice.

Just take a look at the division and how close we are to socialism. Our big government has taken God out of everything. A ruling recently restricted in many of our schools' states that anything pertaining to God could no longer be allowed in the education of our children.

Also, this ruling directed that the display of the Ten Commandments can no longer be displayed in any public or government building. We used to have prayer and a full-time chaplain in our congress as a paid government employee, but that is a thing of the past. The new theme of congress is if you are a Christian, keep it to yourself. Many have pushed that the Bible is a myth, and there is no foundation as a basis for our churches.

Just look at our divided nation and hone in on how love has turned to hate. Even in our congress, hate for those on the opposite political side has resulted in very few bills being passed by participatory vote. Hate for a president has caused a political division that has delayed new bills from passing because of particularization.

In the Bible, King Solomon had a similar problem with his temple. There seemed to be a disorder in the temple that had caused the people to quit trusting in God. If you have read the story, the chaos that came from rejection of God is almost the same thing that has happened to America. Solomon prayed a prayer, asking for God's help. God's answer is quoted on the front cover of this book. But I will repeat it; maybe it will cause those who still believe in God to rumble in a force that will bring the silent majority to life again. Here is God's answer to King Solomon's prayer. And if you know the story, you can confirm it by the Bible. It worked. Prayer changed things. Believe me; we need God's help if we are going to bring America back to *greatness* that gave the people happiness, peace, and joy. America, one nation under God, is also the land of the *free*.

Here is God's answer to the king's prayer to restore his nation back to greatness: "*If my people who are called by my name will humble themselves and pray and seek my face and turn from their wicked ways, I will hear from heaven and will forgive their sins and heal their land*" (2 Chronicles 7:14 NLT). It worked for them, and God stepped in and healed their temple. If it worked for them, it can work for us.

God went on to say that He would listen to every prayer made because He (God) had chosen Solomon's temple and set it apart to be God's home forever. God is saying to America that He has set us apart and that His eyes and heart will always be on America.

Now this should tell all us Christians who are called by His name and live in America to *humble yourself, pray, seek God, and turn from your wicked ways* and then get out and vote, and God will heal our land. Notice this, God will put America back into the hands of the people, but we must do our part. The way I read it, we have to do four things. First and foremost, we have to humble ourselves. Next, and this might be hard for some, we have to pray. Then seek God and run from our wicked ways. At this point, God tells us to stand fast and see the glory of God. However, America seems to have forgotten our heritage, and many don't even know how to *trust in God*, which was the basic foundation passed on to us from our forefathers. They believed so strongly in this that they put those very words on our currency. Look at a dollar bill, and you will find *in God we trust* on every bill and coin minted by and for the United States of America.

Also, since we are already deep into a cultural war between the people and big government, we still must involve ourselves in a fight for our country. *It is time now* for the church to rumble. That means we come together and help the president keep America great. Your vote will go a long way to making America the great nation it has always been.

Don't be confused; we are deep into a cultural war that has now reached a point that there is a strong force to convert this government into socialism. It is evident voters will be called to vote to retain our capitalist form of government or give voters a voice in converting to a socialist government in the next national election.

It has become important for all Americans to realize that not only is there a cultural war between the church (or better explained as the people) and the government (better explained as big government), but there is a continuing spiritual war going on in America between Christians and Muslims. The Spiritual war actually began in the days of Abraham. However, it has recently reached a point that there are now over thirty-one million Muslims who have become citizens in the United States. In this book, we will give insight into both wars and how they are affecting America today.

The key solution is for citizens, Christians, patriots, and all those who have and are enjoying being free to get out your voter's registration and head to the polls.

INTRODUCTION

For decades, there has been a war developing between church and the state, and a form of socialism has been brewing for years in America but has hidden behind big government.' Many of our voters become so lax in their voting that we have allowed government to take "by the people" out of play. If you will recall in our constitution, it says this nation would be a government of the people, by the people, and for the people, and this was always enforced through our voting system.

When I first started writing this book, I had full intentions of giving you some thoughts about how our government had become so big and forceful; many of our rights had been taken away. Voting seems to be so controlled; it seemed to be a waste of time to vote. In fact, in the last election, I was trying to encourage my son to get out and vote, and his reply to me was that it would just be a waste of time. He went on to explain how the voting is so rigged by big government that voting had become a myth.

Up until I began to study the system, I thought I had found the answer to complacency in our society. It all seemed to have started when we began to remove the things of God and any mention of God from our society.

However, after I started digging into it, I learned that there has been a renewal of the holy war, and evidence of this war had already reached into our congress. In the last election, there were a couple of ladies of the Muslim faith elected to the house of representatives. They have become very forceful about turning our government into a socialistic country, and many members of congress have grabbed the idea. What is strange is a socialistic government fits right into the Muslim belief. A couple others joined with the first two congresswomen, and they have put together a group that they called the Squad. Others have joined to support the change. Many of those running for reelection based their campaign on making a change in our form of government to a socialist government.

How the holy war began

Because of the falling away from the study of the Bible, very few know the story about how Abraham had two sons who became leaders of the separate nations. This is recorded in the Bible in the twenty-first chapter of Genesis.

One of the sons, Ishmael, became the father' of the Arab nation, and Isaac became the father' of the nation of Israel. From these two sons, there was a holy war between two religions: Muslim, which developed from Ishmael, and Judaism, which came from Isaac. The Christian belief formulated from the Judaism belief of Abraham and Moses. With the recent influx of Muslims into this country, there has been a renewal of this holy war to rise up in America. This war has combined with the war between church and state and has split this nation in half.

There's a spiritual war (the holy war of Abraham's two sons) and a cultural war between the church (the people) and the state (big government) engulfing our nation. Maybe this book will give a little more understanding to the voters and give an appeal to inspire more Americans to get out and vote.

WE MUST RENEW THE "TRUST IN GOD" OF OUR FOREFATHERS

I also learned that there has been a "falling away" in church attendance, and families were not passing the gospel and the truth about
the Bible on to their children. Unless our children are taught the
truth, they will never know what it is to be free. It was a shock to me
when we first founded this nation. we put a lot of emphasis on sending missionaries to foreign countries to teach them the truth so they
could be set free. Now this has reversed on us, and foreign countries
are sending missionaries to America so we can be set free. America,
where has your sting gone?

Several studies recently showed there has been a decline in Bible
sales.

Today, more and more people no longer have reference Bibles
in their homes like our forefathers had. Maybe President Obama was
right; "America is no longer a Christian nation."

I am hoping this book will at least bring a stirring to the
Christian majority to awaken and realize how close we are to losing
our religious freedom. In this book, I am going to outline what has
been happening in just a few years that has resulted in adding over
thirty-one million Muslims as citizens of this nation.

Just for your information, this book is a book of nonfiction.
And unlike much of the published print of the media today, it does
not contain fake news. Maybe this book will help Christians wake up
and realize that America no longer can be called a Christian nation.
Church, it's time to rumble!

1

AMERICA IS IN A HOLY WAR

For years, there has been a call for term limits of those who are elected to serve in our government. For many years, term limits have always been voted down by congress. As a result, many of our congressmen and congresswomen have retained their appointments, for some over thirty years.

Without term limits, younger, more modern-thinking younger men and woman cannot be voted in to replace the old timers. Without new members, congress members are stagnant and have become so complacent that they forget they are servants of the people. Another problem is our forefathers never intended for those elected to congress to hold that position for thirty years or more. It was assumed that as the nation progressed, new people would be voted in, and a fresh body of congressmen and women would bring new technology and direction. I am getting up in the years myself, and it takes a concentrated effort to adapt to the new world. More than half our congress has been serving as congressmen and women for over ten to thirty years. One congressman just died while still on active duty, and he was first elected into congress thirty-three years ago. It is hard to believe that with all the new technology that a person could be voted in sixteen consecutive times and never be challenged. Maybe my son was right; it does seem to be rigged. He is one of the younger voters, and he has decided that there is no point in him wasting time going to vote. The way he puts it, "You can't fight city hall." Just look at the 2020 presidential election.

One of the things President Trump, our forty-fifth president, tried to correct was to limit the number of terms those serving could serve. Congressmen fought this and even tried twice to impeach the president to keep term limits out of congress.

Many have questioned how congressmen who have spent over thirty years in congress and when they retire have become millionaires. How do you become millionaires with annual salaries of less than two hundred thousand dollars? Maybe this accounts for the huge national debt facing our government. Latest figure for this debt is over twenty-eight trillion dollars. Oh, something most of you may not know, when a congressman or woman retires from congress, even after one term, they retire with full salary.

Even this year, there has been a lot of effort to change the term limits. But since congress has to approve these changes, it has failed to pass. So far, the only term limits that have been voted in is the term of president of the United States. The president can only serve two four-year terms.

Because of no term limits and voter apathy, congressmen have been able to remain in office. Some have served over thirty years. This seemed to slowly cultivate stronger government control and resulted in a bigger and bigger government. In addition, big government has created many power struggles within its ranks. It has reached a point that the people have very little say in governing the country even though our constitution clearly states, "We the people." With the push to take God out of government, many have questioned how we have kept the "in God we trust" on our currency? We no longer turn to God as our forefathers did, nor do we consult the Bible for answers to problems. In the early 2000s, there were a lot of people voicing their concern about the "in God we trust" that was printed on our money. One of the national broadcasting TV networks ran a national survey, asking for people to respond whether to keep "in God we trust" on our currency. They announced that this was one of the largest surveys they had ever run, and the results of this found over 85 percent at that time voted to keep the "in God we trust" on our money. It was reported that this survey revealed, at that time, there were still some 85 percent of those living in America still considered as part of the Christian ranks.

In simple terms, today, the polls taken reveal a lot fewer who profess Christianity than that figure revealed. In fact, many polls record there are now less than 50 percent who account or claim association to the Christian belief.

I mentioned in the introduction that our country is currently in a cultural war between the church and state. Even though this is a war that included the church, it doesn't translate into as Christians being the church. In this case, the word *church* translates to be the "people." I would assume the word *church* was used by our forefathers when they began this country as a Christian nation. However, the cultural war of church is really a war between the people and the big government. Our nation has turned government out to be a power grab between Democrats and Republican. Everything that referred to God has been taken out of our society. Even one president, in the election of 2016, a complete change of power happened when a Republican, Donald Trump, was elected as president of the United States. The Democrats had been in control for nearly a decade; and from all predictions, the Democrats were predicted to pool a landslide in the 2016 elections. Most Democrats had invested all their eggs in one basket.

Actually, this seemed to be the turning point in our country. And when the Republicans were victorious, it caused panic in the ranks of the Democrats. The Democrats had placed all their marbles on a win. And when they lost the election, their world fell apart. Big government had found a way to win; and for some reason, it didn't work this time.

CAN YOU WIN AND STILL LOSE?

In our last election, what happened was very confusing to most voters. Many were unaware that one party could poll the majority of the votes and lose the election. Let me explain what happened. Years back, before computers, when the constitution was first enacted, our forefathers built into the voting system electoral voters. This was put in to keep it a fair system to prevent rigged or dishonest count of the votes. Now I am not a scholar on the constitution so I may not be able to fully explain how it works, but I'll give you a layman's understanding. Again, this ruling was placed in the constitution because at that time the only way to count the votes immediately was by hand. It sometimes took months, or more, to poll the votes. To make it a fair and faster system, our forefathers designed a way to prevent large voting polls from overpowering the system. Under the electoral voting system, every vote was considered by the voting area population. This system called for each state to elect a group of electoral voters who would cast votes by state instead of individual polling. Now understand, I'm not a scholar on the constitution, so if you want more details, you need to get a copy of the constitution and read it for yourself. I understand that each state appointed electoral voters according to the population of the state. In other words, the larger states, like New York, which had several million voters, might have twelve electoral votes, and a state like Rhode Island with a smaller population might only have one electoral vote. To this day, with the computers now counting the votes, I think it would be better that the winner be the one who polled the most popular votes. However, our constitution still operates under the electoral system where the winner is determined by the state electoral voters. Sorry, that is the best I can do to explain it.

In simple terms, here is what happened in the 2016 election. The two parties had Donald Trump running on the Republican ticket and Hillary Clinton on the Democrat. With the new technology, mainly, the computers gave an immediate accounting of votes from the polls. In almost every election, this count can usually determine the winner. Because of the electoral system, which has each state appointing electoral voters with the number coinciding with the state's population, each electoral voter will cast a vote for their state's popular vote. Are you as confused as I am? However, in what little study I have done of the constitution, I have to tell you that there is no doubt in my mind that the constitution is a lot like the Bible and is an inspired writings. This is evidenced by the length of time it has been the law of the land and has been proven over and over.

Back to the election. Hillary polled the most overall votes as counted by the computers, but the votes by area of the electoral board polled Trump as the winner. You know how it goes; some like it hot, and some like it cold. but our nation has adopted and is pledged to operate under our constitution. According to the constitution, Donald Trump legally became the forty-fifth president of the United States.

Well let me tell you, the Democrats did not like it. It took them out of power, and they still have not stopped protesting the results. In fact, my opinion, which I have always heard opinions are a lot like butts—everyone has one, and most of them stink—this has been a big factor in a split down the middle for this Nation. What is sad is neither side has given an inch. In our congress, every vote taken since Mr. Trump, as president, took over, all Democrats vote 100 percent Democrat. And all Republicans vote 100 percent Republican. It is divided right down the middle. If the Bible and history tells a true story, here's what will eventually happen. I'll just tell you what the Bible says will happen. "United we stand, divided we fall." Wow!

A New Nation, Conceived in Liberty and Justice

In 1776, our country voted in a new constitution and agreed to honor and pattern our lives to be governed by this constitution. For some 250 years, we made laws under the direction of this constitution. As a result, we have built and cultivated the greatest and most powerful nation on this continent. Except for a few recent years, just as our forefathers did, we used the Bible as a guide and followed one of its commandments to cultivate a love for our neighbors and to display respect for mankind. We have had times when we had to combine all our efforts to survive a disaster or hard times; but in every case, by pulling together, we always came out victorious. We survived one of the bloodiest civil wars and endured two world wars, hurricanes, and destructive storms, plus other perils. We survived a couple of bombings by other countries that took thousands of lives, with the latest hit being a planned target by radical Muslims who hijacked airplanes and flew them into a couple of our high-rise buildings. But you know what, each time a disaster like this hit America, it caused a coming together of the people, and there were very few who did not reach out in prayer to our Almighty God. I'm not saying I wish this would happen and bring our nation together, but I am saying, it may take another disaster to bring our nation out of this divided state of being we are now facing.

The more I studied where our nation is today, I could see that there is a force that is doing its best to destroy our country. There is more going on than just a war between church and state. As I studied further, I learned that there is an even bigger war taking place in our country that is a renewal of the holy war similar to the war our fore-fathers were enduring when they left England to find a better way of life in America in the 1600s. In England, the holy war was distorting the love and respect for each other, and the same thing happened after the election of 2016 to this nation. It was sad to see how there is a fine line between love and hate when half the population polled together and turned their love for each other into hate. That very thing also happened when the great Civil War broke out.

From all accounts, we, as a nation, have a holy war that seems to have taken away all the trust we have had in God. This war began back in the 1960s when we elected to stop having open prayer in school. From there, we seem to have taken all or anything that had to do with God out of our society. It even caused a national survey asking to remove the "in God we trust" from our money.

When I begin writing about the war between church and state, and as I dug more into it, I found another war that was going on that seem to be contributing toward destruction of our belief in God, and it was well underway toward removing our status as a Christian nation. I researched and learned that in the past fifty years, the citizenship of America has increased from 300,000,000 to 350,000,000. That doesn't seem so bad. However, when I checked it out, I was shocked to learn that during that time, 31,000,000 of that increase was mostly Muslims.

Recently, I drove by a new church in my neighborhood, and I read the sign telling what kind of church it was, and the name started with *Ishmael*. If you haven't heard this name before, he was the bas-tard son of Abraham.

It didn't take me long to figure out where a lot of the hate that is developing in America is coming from. In case you didn't know, the Muslims' Bible or book they live by is called the Koran. I got one and read a little of it, and I can tell you it is opposite to our Bible. Our Bible has love for our fellowman and even our enemies, but the Koran is just the opposite, it is full of hate. Just as an example, I read that if you are not a Muslim, you are an infidel. It went on to say that, as a Muslim, you are directed to kill all infidels. In fact, it instructs the Muslims that the more infidels they kill, the higher status they will have in their heaven.

Here is a big part of the problem. Americans seem not to connect to a church like they used to. Because of both parents having to work just to make a living, families don't have time to go to church. In the earlier days of our society, most of us attended some form of worship and took our children with us. One of the most important things in life was to teach our children about God first and then give allegiance to our flag and nation. Nowadays we seem to have violated one of the oldest commandments: If it ain't broke, don't fix it. Maybe that is what happened. We tried to fix the church.

This might be a good time to tell you a story my dad shared with me about what he and a couple of other guys did that completely disrupted the local church community. Going to church was a lot different in the early days. No matter what it took, families took their families to church, usually on Sunday. And if they lived close to the church, most of them would go to church on Sunday night and once during the week. However, this was when they didn't have TV or other meetings, and the church was a good way to fellowship. Maybe that is a lot of our problem today; we don't take time to fellowship with our fellowman. Today we don't even know our next-door neighbor.

The community my dad lived in was small but was a large farm ing community. Each farmhouse was several miles apart. Each farm was usually five or more miles apart and sometimes more than five miles from the church. In addition to serving as a church, the building was usually used as a community meeting place where they had combined meetings for both church and the community. On Sunday, the farmers would load up the buggies with family, most of them had several children, and they headed for church. As I said, most of them lived several miles away, and buggies and wagons were not fast movers. It usually took at least an hour to make the journey. Keep in mind, they did not have cell phones or any other means of communication. They knew each other from church because they made Sunday's church a full day of visiting with their different families. They had Sunday school on Sunday mornings and a praise service on Sunday night. They all took food and put it together and dined all day, played cards and dominoes, and the youngsters played games together. On Sunday night, the parents would bed the children down in the buggies and wagons, and the adults stayed for the evening church worship as long as they wanted to.

On the night, my dad and his friends played a prank. The kids had all been bedded down and asleep in the wagons, and church service was in full swing. About four of the teenagers, including my dad, decided to switch the children from one wagon to another. To me, it was a cruel trick. Here is what happened.

After church, the parents all boarded their buggies and headed home after a full day of activities. It was getting late, and none of them thought to check their children who were fast asleep in the wagons. Keep in mind, most of them lived at least five miles from the church. It wouldn't have been much of a problem today; but back then, they did not have a way to communicate with other families. The telephone had not been invented; and being farmers, they lived miles away from the others' families. When they got home, just imagine, they learned they had someone else's kid. The child was too small to know the people, couldn't tell anyone where they lived, and there was no way to determine where they lived—no cell phones, no telephones, and no idea who they could contact for help. They had to bed the kid down and wait till the next day to solve the problem.

Think with me! What made it worse, if your child was in someone else's wagon, you had no way of knowing who the child's parents were. According to Dad, this caused a panic in the entire community. He learned that most of them just put the children to bed and later contacted each other until they finally got their child back. Dad said he and the other boys never got caught, but they had to walk softly for weeks. I can image not having telephones, cell phones, or any other means of communication, only horse-drawn carriages and no cars. And it being nighttime, I would have been in a state of panic.

LIKE IT OR NOT, WE ARE IN A HOLY WAR

Most Americans have no concept that America is involved in a holy war. In fact, very few have the knowledge that it was Muslims who hijacked and flew the airplanes into the twin towers on 9/11, taking some three thousand men, women, and children's lives, nor does anyone know if this was an act of war or was just a terrorist group, but we do know they were Muslims.

It might be a little easier to understand how those people who had relatives killed in 9/11 could easily turn their love to hate for Muslims. Also, you might be hard-pressed to accept a Muslim who had become an American citizen and was now your neighbor.

It is hard to realize how much hate had engulfed our nation, not just for Muslims. But it has reached a point that we even hate our neighbors. It seems to be just the opposite from what Christ told his followers; that is to love your neighbors as yourself.

This hate that has gripped this country has not only taken away the love for each other, but it has cut into the respect we have for each other. It is sad that Americans have lost respect for our leaders, our servicemen, firemen, policemen, pastors, and almost all those who protect our nation. We used to remove our hats, place our hand over our heart, and salute the national flag—no more! I remember when we held up our president in reverence; and nowadays, he is called a liar and other names so rude that I can't repeat them. I also remember when we had respect for our churches, and we referred to them as a house of worship. There was a time in our history when outlaws would seek protection by entering the church sanctuary. Many times, even the law enforcement would not enter the church to apprehend the outlaws.

What is even sadder, we seem to have created a spirit of apathy toward God and things that are related to God. This all seemed to happen when we removed public prayer from our schools. That was back in the 1960s. And since then, everything has moved to taking God out of our culture. We even made a law that the Ten Commandments could not be displayed in or on any public buildings. We seem to have developed a form of godliness that carries no power with it. I'd like to inject a little warning to those of you who believe in the God our forefathers taught to love and respect. There is a Scripture in the Bible (2 Timothy 3:1–5) which warns us to be careful and be aware that we are living in the last days when we reach the state of apathy that has developed in America. In fact, let me quote this directly from the Living Bible translation. It says, "That in the last days there will be very difficult times. For people will love only themselves and their money. They will be boastful and proud, scoffing at God, disobedient to their parents, and ungrateful. They will consider nothing sacred. They will be unloving and unforgiving, they will slander others and have no self-control; they will be cruel and have no interest in what is good. They will betray their friends, be reckless, be puffed up with pride, and love pleasure rather than God. They will act as if they are religious, but they will reject the power that could make them godly" (NLT).

Understand, this is not written by one of our news reporters who have been known to write fake news, but this is taken directly from the Word of God. As I look around, I can see that this fits America like a glove. I have to believe we are approaching the last days!

It is easy to understand why so many have lost their love and respect for each other. There is profound falling away from the *trust in God* that our forefathers worked so hard to establish in this beautiful country so we might know the truth. Again, drawing from the Bible, the truth will set you free.

When I was younger and started driving, there was a theme given to all drivers that curiosity breeds curiosity. Unlike it is today, when you needed to change lanes, the driver in the other lane would slow down and wave you in front. Drivers today don't know how to slow down and let you in, but they sure know how to honk the horn. If you pull in front of someone today, you are taking your life in your own hands. I don't know how many are killed in road rage each year, but there is a bunch. It seems that everyone hates his fellowman. If you accidently cut someone off, about all you can do is pray they don't have a gun. We have taken God and everything pertaining to Him out of our country. We have started electing Muslims to our congress. These are the people who hated us so much that they hijacked two of our airplanes and flew them into our skyscrapers, killing over three thousand of our men, women, and children.

This might be a good place to put a word in for the Holy Bible. I realize, most of you don't even own a Bible. The old timers used to have one in every room in the house. Nowadays we have one in every hand by way of cell phones, but most don't know that. Every cell phone has an app that allows you to call up different versions of the Bible. Try calling it up if you haven't; or better yet, call it up and read it. You might be surprised how interesting it is to read. What I like is it tells me of the past. It talks about what is going on in the world today and gives you an insight on what happens to you when you die. For example, did you know there is a scripture in the Bible that will tell you to love and respect your fellowman? Also, recorded in Matthew 6:24 (NLT), the Bible confirms most of our country's problems are motivated more by the love of money than by love and respect for our fellowman. In the Bible, it says, "No man can serve two masters. For you will hate one and love the other, or be devoted to one and despise the other." It goes on to say that "You cannot serve both God and money" (NLT).

Our forefathers, who started this nation, used the Bible and commandments from the Bible when they laid the foundation for this nation. In fact, it was from the Bible that our forefathers created and framed displays of the Ten Commandments. I often wonder why we progressed in life to a point that we digressed to removing everything that relates or pertains to the Bible from our society. I do know this: We lost a lot of stature when we made the rule that there could no longer be prayers given in school. Then our congress voted to pass a law to force removal of all monuments portraying or displaying the Ten Commandments from government or public properties. Then we took away the last commandment, which was mostly a moral law that Christ gave to us on how to live and enjoy each other. Here is what Christ said; it is recorded in John 13:34–35 (NLT): "So now, I am giving you a new commandment: Love each other, just as I have loved you, you should love each other." There are so many good and positive things in the Bible. if you don't read them, you'll miss out on a lot. Did you know, the Bible tells us to think on those things that are pure and positive? It even tells us how to have an abundant life here on earth.

Let me ask you a question: What has caused our congress to be so divided to a point that the Democrats and the Republicans don't even speak to each other? Do you feel that is love for each other, or does it tend to be more of a hate for one another? In fact, it seems to me, there is no love displayed for each other from both sides. Why would that be a surprise to anyone, since we have worked so hard to remove God from our government that no one knows that the Bible tells us to love one another? What I am saying is to retain our greatness. We must once again take out our Bibles and, as our forefathers did, return to a "*love for each other*" and create a right spirit toward our fellowman. Nowadays, it seems to be hard to love one another. There is a general hate that has engulfed our nation. In a study of the Muslim's bible or the Koran, I noticed it was lined with nothing but hate. Most of that hate is directed to all those who are not of the Muslim belief. I did learn from my brief study that, as a Christian, I am an infidel to the Muslims in their bible, and they are instructed to destroy or kill me. When you go as an American to the polls to vote, keep in mind that if you vote to replace our government with a socialist government, you are voting to further a government that caters to the Muslim belief. Personally, I choose to stay alive and enjoy the freedom I get from being an American.

Since our country is divided between two political parties, it might be good time to start returning our nation back to being free by trusting in the God of our forefathers and rekindling respect for each other. Turn our hate back to love, and pick up our Bibles and learn the truth. There is a scripture that tells us that *the truth will set us free.* You know, our forefathers must have read this when they started this land of the free.

If we could just start living by the verses that are recorded in Philippians 4:8 (NLT), it says, "Fix your thoughts on what is true and honorable and right. Think about things that are pure and lovely and admirable. Think on things that are excellent and worthy of praise." If everyone would live like this, we sure might cultivate a lot more friends. At another place in the Bible, it says we should love our enemy. I don't know if we could get the Democrats and Republicans to ever agree to this, but we might get some of them to wipe the dust off their Bibles and review what our forefathers taught us. Or if all else fails, encourage them to pull out a dollar bill or a handful of change and read the "in God we trust" that is imbedded on each coin and printed on the dollar bills. It seems that our forefathers made great efforts to ensure that our society was built on a trust in God, and it could be that trust has contributed to making this country a great nation.

How could anyone who has experienced the freedom and liberty that America offers push to change to a form of government that takes away the freedom and liberty that America offers? Unless they have come to be missionaries for the Muslim faith, why should we sit back and let them push America in socialism?

It is hard to believe that so many immigrants who have come to America for a better life, especially those of the Muslim belief, are trying to change America to a different culture. It just doesn't compute.

Let me give you a little history on how our laws and beliefs have changed toward those who have immigrated to our country. In 1952, congress passed a bill that became law that stated there would be no Muslims elected to the congress of the United States. This law remained in force until the 1960s, when several senators, which included Senators Joe Biden and John McCain, introduced and passed a bill to repeal the1952 law to allow *Muslim* citizens to be elected to serve in congress. Well in a recent election, there were four

Muslim women, who call themselves the Squad, who were elected to serve as congresswomen in the house of representatives. These four started immediately pushing to convert America's government into a socialist government. In fact, a couple of them even wore their native dress. Oh, what a tangled web we weave! *It's time to rumble!*

Pray for Venezuela

Let me take a moment to give you an example of a country that once was a democratic republic that was taken over by a dictator and is now classified as a socialist government. I almost cry when I see how this country was once an oil-rich nation, flowing with milk and honey, and now is a country of starving people with national poverty that doesn't provide enough food to feed their people. This nation is the country of Venezuela, which was a republic of South America. Venezuela was a republic with more oil, per capital, than most countries that size. Venezuelans had formed a culture that shared the wealth of oil and at one time was known as one of the most prosperous nations in the country. The United States was one of the first and closest allies that Venezuela cultivated. This proved to be a very profitable union, which resulted in Venezuela opening a chain of gasoline stations throughout the United States. If I remember right, these stations were called city services. During its heyday, Venezuela was considered one of the wealthiest small nations in the world. Venezuela at that time, and because of its size, often called on the US to help ward off dictatorship.

Venezuela constantly had many forces trying to convert the nation to be a socialist nation. Through a rigged election, a socialist was voted in. He rose and took over the nation as a dictator of the country. He took command of the armed forces and established his dictatorship as the ruling force for the country. Anyone who disagreed with or chose to go against his rule was put to death. He began to make laws that took control of the government and rule of the country away from the people. Come time to vote, he had manipulated the voting system to where the votes of the people no longer counted and, through a false count, was put into power. As president, he controlled the armed forces and declared himself dictator of the socialistic government. In just a short time, he owned and controlled all the oil and its reserves. And instead of the people sharing in the wealth of the nation, they became subjects of the government. Next move, he took away all guns owned by the people, and they were left with no means to protect themselves. They worked their crops, but the government confiscated the rewards, and the people were given just enough to keep from starving. The people no longer could own any property, and they became subjects of the government (dictator). America no longer bought their oil, and all their service stations were closed or sold to another company.

Then the dictator died. Another strong man took over. He also let the people vote in a rigged election designed and set him up to win. By this time, the people had lost all control and decided to revolt and take back their country. They chose a leader and voted to go to war to retrieve their country. They asked the United States to help, but America was very much in its own problems at that time and couldn't help much. Very few people were allowed into the country because the dictator had closed the country where no foreign country could get in to help. The army was still under the command of the dictator, and the people had no guns to fight with. Remember, they were all confiscated by the former dictator. And when people revolted, without any guns to fight with, they lost big time. It is sad to say that things went from bad to worse. There are thousands and thousands starving to death in Venezuela today. If you are a Christian reading this book, please say a prayer for the people of Venezuela.

In the Beginning
God Created

No longer can we know if the news is true or fake because journalists write more fake news nowadays than they do the truth. About the only way you can know the truth is to read the Bible. Most of us don't have Bibles anymore, and most of our news is false, at least the daily papers publish mostly editorials, so people just watch TV. People used to buy Bibles. And for hundreds of years, the Bible had been the bestselling book and each year sold more than any other books. There was no question that it was the true Word of God; and in the old days, there was usually a Bible in every room in the house.

Newest thing lately is the Bible is a myth. (Maybe not the newest thing, but that theory has popped up a lot lately). It just proves that man is never satisfied even when he finds something that gives him the truth. Man has been trying to prove the Bible is not the truth mainly because it gives an accounting for how man was created by God, and it tells of a *life* hereafter. *Butt Man*—I wrote it like that because man has finally proved he is a butt. Really, God made man to think for himself and gave him a brain that seeks out the truth. In the end, he is not smart enough to do what the Bible tells him to do: "Seek first the kingdom of God and all these things will be added unto you." Doctor Luke, in the book of Luke 17:21 (KJV), said, "The kingdom of God is within you." In another place, it is recorded that if you serve Christ, He will give you an abundant life. As an American, ask yourself why we are so divided and confused. Our forefathers built it and taught us and even put it on our money to trust in God, even directed us to the Bible which says it like this: Trust in the Lord with all your heart, and lean not to your own understanding, in all your ways acknowledge Him (God) and He will direct your path (Proverb 3:5–6 KJV).

Before I leave this thought, I would like to pass on to you something that was penned by a man: "You have to believe in something, or you will fall for anything." I don't know who wrote that, but I do know my father quoted it to me often. Another thing my father taught me is, "if it ain't broke, don't fix it." We were given a good foundation by those forefathers who made their way over to this country and passed on the land of the *free* to us where we could have an abundant life and live in the greatest country in the world. Being the dummies we are, even though it wasn't broke, we had to fix it. Santa is laughing, *ha, ha, ho*…Merry Christmas.

I grew up in a culture that claimed the Bible was the infallible Word of God and was the base that our forefathers had brought to this country. If it was the most famous book ever written and was a book that anyone who would read it could find the truth. Most homes, when this nation was first started, had several Bibles, and many had a Bible in each room. In America, the Bible has been on the best-seller list since the list was invented. There has never been a book that can give you as true of an accounting of life as the Bible and can teach you more about life than any college or teacher.

Sorry, but I am a Gideon, one of those people who put Bibles in the motels, nursing homes, hospitals, and other public places, so I had to get a word in for our Gideon brothers who have planted billions of Bibles throughout this country and foreign nations. This new nation voiced a freedom of religion and pledged to the Republic a freedom that is unmatched by any other nation. Most of the nations, at the time of the signing of our constitution, were socialist governments, usually under dictatorship.

Now that America Is a Big Government

I want to take you back to how this country was started under a three class system, which is the making of a capitalistic form of government. This type of government is a culture where all the people are given voting rights to determine the majority rule of the government. When our nation adopted a constitution it set up a Christian nation that would also be a nation that was operated by the people, for the people, and of the people. In order to enact a right to vote, our forefathers had to establish a system to give each person an equal vote, regardless of a person's wealth or stature. They chose to establish a three-class system of the rich, the middle class, and the poor. Under our constitution, the middle class proved to be the majority.

Since this class was determined to be the majority of the people, it also became the ruling class of this nation that we call the republic of the United States of America. This class, as a majority class, is charged with paying more taxes and, through an established voting system, has become the operating force of the government. In the past couple of decades, we have slowly been moving toward a two-class system where the middle class is disappearing. It seems that if you live in America today, you are either rich or poor. What is sad about this is we no longer have anyone left in the working class. When our country first started, we pushed for children to obtain a twelfth-grade education. We established a public educational system that required our children to attend public schooling without charge. A public education was available to all children who were living in America, and this education was paid for through our tax revenue. In other words, a child's education was free to all children who resided in America. This system was designed to give each child a basic education. In grades one through six, the kids were taught the basics of reading, writing, and arithmetic. I remember a song that many of us used to sing. It went something like this: "school days, school days, dear old golden rule days, reading and writing and arithmetic, taught to the tune of the hickory stick." After the first six grades, which were called elementary school, the children were graduated to junior high school. These grades included the seventh, eighth, and ninth grades. Next was high school—grades ten, eleven, and twelve. In high school, they taught classes that centered more on preparing for jobs after graduation. In fact, some of the schools were converted to technical schools that taught basic skills to qualify their students for outside jobs after graduation. States, along with some private universities, offered higher education for professional training to students who wanted to enter the professional workforce, such as doctors, lawyers, executives, and other professionals. These schools were offered by colleges and universities, and the students were charged an enrollment fee if they wanted to continue this part of their education.

For over two hundred years, America has been known to have the best and most effective educational system in the world. It was designed to provide education to the rich, the middle class, and the poor.

After World War II, when our servicemen and women began to return home, most of them had to start life all over again. A lot of them, who were called to serve in the war, were farmers and ranchers who lived in rural areas prior to the war. After the war, factories began to open up, and most of those who lived in the rural areas prior to the war, chose to move to the city and took jobs in the city. City life, with quiet and peaceful neighborhoods, began to spring up all over the country. Most of the new cities were midsize and became examples of what our forefathers intended to be when they establish communities to be a part of the life in the United States of America. These communities became thriving towns with a main street and a church of different religions springing up on every corner. They sent their children to school every day where they were taught to respect and honor the flag as a symbol of freedom. In fact, before school started each morning, they recited a pledge to the flag and gave honor to America as "one nation under God, indivisible, with liberty and justice for all." This proved to be a time when God's blessings were being poured out on all Americans. It proved <u>to</u> be the most fruitful time ever for America. Factories flourished, and cities grew to become huge metropolis.

America began to prosper, and many in the middle class or work ing class prospered individually and learned how great it was to live in a country of the free. Many middle-class citizens become doctors, lawyers, and such, and many prospered and moved from the working class to the rich. Over the years, the middle class has been fading out, and America is on the way to becoming a two-class country, the rich and the poor. Another way of saying it can be expressed by the cliche was that it was used by children playing cowboys and Indians when those chosen to be Indians all wanted to be a chief. The cliche was "all Chiefs and no Indians." In America, everyone wanted to be the doctor, and no one wanted to be the patient.

This change in our class system has caused several changes in our country. It caused our educational system to move away from tech-nical schools where our kids no longer got jobs after finishing high school, but now they take out a loan and go to college. Nowadays, almost every student elects to continue their education by enrolling in a college or university. Another change that has taken place is we can't find workers to fill jobs in the workforce. Results are, many of our manufacturing companies had to move overseas to find cheaper workers. There was a time when everyone in the labor wanted to start at the top level and draw an executive salary. Without a labor force America has moved closer and closer to socialism where everyone works for the government.

Back to the Holy War of Ishmael and Isaac

What has happened in the past twenty years is we have added another thirty million to our citizenship roll. This thirty million that has been added to our citizenship roll has mostly been members of the Muslim faith. The Muslim faith operates under a socialist form of government or dictatorship. They have infiltrated our nation to a point that they have built mosques where Muslims worship their god. Their name gives a different distinction of identity by using the name Ishmael in name of the mosque. For those of you who are not familiar with the name Ishmael, in the Bible, he was Abraham's bastard son that Abraham fathered with Sarah's handmaiden, Hagar. (If some of you Bible scholars want to look this up, you might have to look it up under the name of Abram and Sarai since this event took place before God changed their names to Abraham and Sarah.)

I would like to give you a little background and a personal knowledge I have on how Muslims have been infiltrating into this country for the last seventy or more years. In the 1960s, I owned a business that required me to travel. I mostly traveled in the four corners of the United States. At that time, there were a lot of smaller motels owned by individual Americans. In the late 1950s, a lot of Americans were choosing to take family vacations by driving to different parts of the country and taking in the beauty of those spacious skies and fruited plains, which make up the combined beauty of America. This became a way of life and fit right in with two-week vacations provided by their employer. So they packed up the car and spent two weeks driving and found a motel (sometimes they were called *courts*) to find a place to sleep. Usually, they picked a motel that was owned by one of their fellow Americans; and in most cases, the travelers learned a lot from the owners about the local town and cities. Since they had to locate a café to eat the evening meal, they knew the owner would know where to dine.

At the same time, this travel provided a wealth of knowledge and education to their children. Also, they got to know why a lot of Americans had chosen to find a peaceful and different life in small-town America. Actually, this was a time when America was beginning to reclaim life from a devastating World War that had rocked the very foundation of life in America.

What had happened was many of the motel owners found that owning and operating a motel proved a good way of life and a good place to raise a family.

By the 1960s, most of the owners were getting up in age, and their kids had moved out. Most of them had reached an age where retirement was near, and with all their customers telling them of their travels, many put their motels on the market to sell.

In my travels with my job, I liked to end my day a little earlier so I could relax a little before supper. For those of you who may not know what supper is, it is the old-time way of expressing what we now call dinner. During that time of relaxing, I usually picked one of the motels owned by individuals and got acquainted with them. It proved a nice way to swap ideas and small talk about life and families. I learned that most of them had a good life but were tired and ready to stop cleaning rooms.

It wasn't long into my travels that it seemed almost all of a sudden, I began to see a few of the motel's marquees had "American owned" on them. This began to appear more and more. One night, I chose one of the motels that had this on their sign, and the owner shared with me that most of the motels were being bought out by foreign countries. It seemed that many of the motels were being bought by a couple of foreign nations. After the foreign country purchased a motel, they carefully selected a young married couple from their country to manage them. Most of the couples were very young, had just gotten married, and were ready to start having children.

It didn't take long for the travelers to get the word out that most of the small motels were not maintained like they had been in the past. The rooms were not cleaned, and the management had changed. A lot of unpleasant changes were taking place. In no time, you could hardly find a place that was still American owned. That was why the American owned was being placed on the marquees; it reflected a cleaner motel. I finally had to give in and stay in one of the motels that was foreign owned because, in the small towns, this was the only motel available. However, I still took time to visit with the new owners, and everyone I talked to seemed to have the same story. Here is what I learned.

I learned that as far back as the 1960s, Muslims had put a concentrated effort to plant young married couples of the Muslim belief to come to America as a form of missionaries to America. At that time, I never gave any thought to what was going on. I had no idea that America had a law where any child physically born in America would automatically become a natural citizen of the United States. What that means is even if the parents are not American citizens, every child born to them while visiting or immigrating to America becomes a naturalized citizen of this nation.

While visiting with the new motel owners, I learned a little more about these couples and what a sweet deal they had. After a certain number of years, they became owners of the motel they managed. They had a certain number of children born in this country. As I stated before, each of these children automatically became American citizens. By the time I came around, many of them already had several children. Just recently, after learning that our census polls showed there were thirty-one million Muslims listed as American citizens, it jogged my memory. I quickly recalled that it was in the early 1960s when I had encountered those foreign-owned motels. It works a little like what happened to me when I was a youngster. Someone gave me a couple of rabbits, and by the time I turned around, I had twenty rabbits. A year later, I had so many rabbits that they couldn't fit on the two acres my parents had. I remembered almost every couple at the motels I visited, and almost all said their goal was to have at least ten kids. Now add up all the Muslim immigrants and those who were able to achieve citizenship by other means and include all the Muslim children born at the motels then figure sixty years to grow. After all, from the 1960s to the 2020s, with that sixty years, and if just one thousand motels at ten children, in ten years, ten thousand times sixty years would amount to six hundred thousand. If each of those had ten kids, it's no longer rabbits we are talking about, but all those who were born in America automatically become citizens of the United States because of the natural birth clause. Then throw some one hundred thousand who became citizens illegally, and you are getting close to thirty million. I know we are not dealing with rabbits, but if they each had ten children, next year they should number fifty million. Before you know it, *wow*! Minority becomes majority. Don't take this to heart, but at least think about it in terms of what could be happening to us as a Christian nation.

Oh, Holy Night, Without a Wake-Up Call?

When our forefathers chose to establish this nation as a nation under one God, they elected to operate as a capitalist form of government. This government became a Christian nation and was a government of the people, which was the opposite of a socialist form of government. They introduced the Holy Bible and used this Bible as a foundation for building this great nation. This country has, for over three hundred years, been cultivating a society of Christian people who chose to print on their currency "in God we trust." Only in the past couple of decades has this trust in God been challenged to a point that questioned this nation as being a Christian nation. It is hoped that this book will serve as a *wake-up* call to all Christian patriots, along with the conservatives, to come out and express their choice through voting.

Because of the two wars, the war between church and state and the holy war, Christians have retreated to their closets. They no longer attend church, no longer worship God, and have backed away from public service under the name of Jesus Christ. When our forefathers established this nation, the church body made up the majority of the government. Nowadays the church has little say in government, and even sadder, not many Christians show up to vote anymore. One of the largest reasons this book is being published is to call out the Christians to come alive in the next election and once again take control of government. Huge steps have been made to make this country great again, but it will never happen without the help of those who profess Christianity. If there was ever a time when the voice of the people needs to be heard, it is now. There is a force that is rising up to overthrow this government and convert our government to socialism. *Awake, America. Don't slumber in your waking, but get up and make your voice be heard.* One of the greatest gifts our forefathers left with us was our system of voting. It is one of the best things that help keep our people in control of our nation.

I can tell you, if you like the freedom we have in this country, all true Americans will seek the truth and will have the faith to believe that the truth will come forward, and we will be set free. Thanks to those brave pilgrims who rode out the perils of the ocean in a make-shift ship who left England to find a freedom of worship. In fact, let me paint you a picture of that cold winter morning that these brave souls left for us to remember and be ever thankful.

This nation all started when a group of godly worshipers from England were being persecuted by the ruling forces, and some were even put to death because they refused to conform to the established form of worship. As an act of salvation, this group pooled their resources and acquired a ship and stocked it full of supplies to last them for several weeks and made their way across the ocean.

They had heard of a land that was discovered by an Italian sailor in the 1400s. It is believed that those involved in this group had been studying in the New Testament of the Holy Bible and had read about how a Savior came down from heaven to save mankind from their sins. It told the story that God, who had created man, sent his only begotten Son to die on a cross, and those who believed that he was the Son of God could become pan of the new kingdom of God. In the Old Testament, it was prophesied that God would come down to earth and set up a kingdom on earth to reign forever. In the New Testament, this kingdom would be set up in a place called heaven. After they had confirmed to themselves that this was the true Word of God, they began to share this belief with others. The New Testament belief was accepted by many, and many believed that Jesus the Christ was the Savior of man. Those who were confessed believers of the Judaism belief considered this new belief heresy because this Savior of the New Testament was referred to as the Messiah. This new belief of the New Testament claimed that this was the Messiah, that the Old Testament believers were looking to come back and set up a kingdom of utopia on earth. The old timers did not accept that Christ was the Son of God that they had been looking for Him to return as a King, not as a baby born in a manger. The doubt sparked the pilgrims persecution when other religious groups considered this belief a false doctrine. A holy war broke out.

As Americans, I know most of you old timers know this story better than I do. I gave my version, and those of you who have never heard this story, get yourself a copy of the Holy Bible and read it for yourself. There is one thing I always tell those who do not believe the simple part of accepting Jesus Christ as your Savior, you might want to read on and learn what we are saved from. The Bible goes on and tells what happens to man after he dies. In my reading of the Bible, I learned that if I did not accept Christ as my Savior, when I die, I will be cast or thrown into a lake of fire and will burn forever and ever. The Bible tells us that when we die and this life is over, because God created us, we will live forever. If I do accept Christ as my Savior, I will go to that heaven that I mentioned as a utopia and live as a king forever and ever. Here is the way I look at it: If there is a hell and there is a heaven, and all I have to do is accept Jesus Christ as my Savior, from what I have heard, I choose heaven. Actually, it is not even a choice for me.

Better than me telling you, do yourself a favor and get yourself a Bible. It won't cost very much, and it will tell you about life hereafter. One other point, when you read the Bible, be sure and read how Christ can change your life to a new abundant life, and at the same time, God will give you a peace beyond your understanding. In closing, when you get your Bible, look up the book of Galatians 5:22. It says, "When the Holy Spirit controls our lives, the Holy Spirit will produce this kind of fruit in us: love, joy, peace, patience, kindness, goodness, faithfulness, gentleness and self-control" (NLT). Here's the way I look at it: Isn't love much better than all the hate and killing each other? All of this comes free by just accepting Christ as your Savior. That's my story, and I'm sticking to it!

Back to the pilgrims, they knew they had to find a way to escape. They read in the Bible how the Israelites had been under a similar persecution, and God led them to a promised land. In their search, they found writings of how a new land across the ocean had been discovered. They all gathered and started making plans to make their way to this distant land. The more they prayed, the more they cultivated within their belief was a promised land that was flowing with milk and honey, just like God promised to the Israelites. They loaded the boat and set sail to find a land that flowed with milk and honey. After a couple of weeks, they saw what looked like a small glimpse of land, and they knew they had found it. By that afternoon, they could make out a large island of land. And by dark, they found a large rock, which we now call Plymouth Rock and cast anchor.

I can picture in my mind how they all gathered together, and one suggested that they call this land America. The song writer put it this way: "America, America, God shed his grace on thee, and crown thy good with brotherhood, from sea to shining sea!"

Turned out, they did find their promised land and cultivated that land to become the greatest nation on earth. This nation has flowed with justice, liberty, and the pursuit of happiness for over four hundred years, endured famine, earthquakes, natural disasters, wars, and even a great Civil War. Its flag still flies high and, for over two hundred years, has been one nation under God. It stands today as a symbol of freedom. Even though one of its presidents declared that it was no longer a Christian nation, they still hold to the basic teaching that Jesus Christ is their Savior, and we are still one nation under God. God bless America.

REMOVE GOD AND THE TEN COMMANDMENTS

Since I have started a history lesson, I might as well continue and give those of you who have not been taught what has caused this nation's greatness. There is a movement in our country today that wants to take past history out of our thoughts, leave us no memory of the past. As an example, in the 1960s, a woman pushed and was successful in getting prayer removed from our public schools. Just a few years back, our government made laws that ordered all displays of the Ten Commandments or any mention of God could no longer be displayed in any federal or public buildings. There has been a concentrated effort to take God out of our culture. I mentioned earlier how one of the presidents, in a speech to a foreign nation, made the declaration that America was no longer a Christian nation.

This is so different from what it was when I started school. I remember from the first day in September 1942, when I walked up the stairs and found my room in a small school in Nocona, Texas. The first thing that happened was I heard a voice come from a loud speaker. We all bowed in prayer and prayed for our country. The very next thing, the teacher had us all to stand and recite the Pledge of Allegiance to the flag. If I remember it right, this pledge went like this: "I pledge allegiance to the flag of the United States of America, and to the republic for which it stands (at that time, one nation under God was later added) indivisible, with liberty and justice for all." I understand, some of the schools still recite this, but most no longer do. We no longer pass on to our children this part of our heritage. But when I went to school, it was a big part of our education. It is said that some of the public schools no longer teach our heritage, and many have dropped it from their curriculum. It not only is being taken out of our schools but is being removed from our government. In the communities now, by law, they have removed statues, flags, and other things pertaining to the confederates of the Civil War.

Back to that group of pilgrims who endured hardships and strife to settle and start this nation. From the time they landed at Plymouth Rock, they brought and passed on a new way of life that is recorded in John 3:16 of the New Testament: For God so loved the world, that he gave his only son, so that everyone who believes in him will not perish but have eternal life (NLT).

SET THE ANCHOR—
WE FOUND OUR
PROMISED LAND

I can picture how excited they must have been when they got up that morning and gathered on the bow of that ship, singing that old song: "Amazing grace, how sweet the sound that saved a wretch like me. I once was lost, but now I'm found, was blind but now I see." They looked out and saw a thin covering of snow that reflected a glow of beauty with a background of trees that helped make a picture of milk and honey without cows. Then all of a sudden, there appeared a band of what looked like a very curious group of people. This caused these pilgrims to wonder if these people were aggressive. There seemed to be no aggression, and they seemed to be very friendly. Several of them held up their hands in a friendly manner. Bottom line, the pilgrims made friends with the natives and later called them Indians. Even with a language barrier, they were able to explain to the Indians that they had traveled many miles in a ship and had very little food remaining. They learned that these Indians were very friendly and seemed to be civilized in their own way. In fact they even gave them some fresh carrots and greens they had grown from their gardens. The pilgrims had things like clocks, mirrors, knives, and coins that they traded for food. History records that they joined with these Indians and had the first Thanksgiving with their new friends. That could be made up; and like I have done in describing the first landing, it could be a true story. Either way, it is recorded that they did include their new friends in their culture. I don't doubt that they invited them to worship with them.

It took very little time for the pilgrims to build a place of worship, which they used as a meeting place to discuss business and share the Word of God. In addition, they established their first colony and named it Jamestown.

The colony grew, and soon there were thirteen colonies. In 1776, these thirteen colonies joined together and formed a new nation that became the republic of the United States of America.

Every pilgrim was confirmed in their faith. They made sure to include the Bible, as a true Word of God. And as the nation grew, they took time daily to worship and fellowship and teach their children the gospel of Jesus Christ.

When they wrote the constitution of this great nation, history shows that all those who were involved in putting the constitution together were professed Christians. In fact, four of the writers were ordained as ministers of the gospel. As each colony was started, the local government was formulated under Christian bylaws. I'm sure that those forefathers were careful to relate how a holy war in England motivated them to find a new home in America. If we don't teach our children about how much religion is part of our heritage, they will grow up not knowing many of the hardships our forefathers endured just to establish this nation as one nation under God.

Between the war of church and state and the holy war, Christianity is slowly being taken away from this nation. Going to church no longer is included in our activities, and things of God are being taken out of our government. Prayer, one of the things that caused this nation to become great, has moved way down on the totem pole and is not practiced much anymore. I will say that when I go out to eat, I do see many bowing their heads and saying a prayer before they eat. However, I also live in the Bible Belt. For those who might be reading this book who do not know what the Bible Belt is, it is an area or city that Christians used to call a city that had a church on every corner. These seem like little things, and it's true, it doesn't seem to be a big deal. But so many little things that refer to God or Christianity are fading away.

Christians, awake, arise, and once again be counted. You are still the majority, and let's come out and show we are still around. It might mean you should get back in church and take your children to Sunday school. But if we don't do it, we might wind up losing our freedom of religion. I like that we have created a new nation, conceived in liberty, and dedicated to proposition that all people are created equal. The Bible says, we are all created equal, so let's stand up and testify. We need to get rid of big government and once again recreate a government of the people, by the people, and for the people. Get back in church and worship the Lord. This might be a good time for us to do what God told Solomon to tell the people to do to heal their land. Remember, God told the people to pray and seek God, humble themselves, and turn from their evil ways.

Throughout the past four hundred years, America has had to stand tall to recover from all the hardships of wars, disasters, and storms of life that America has had to endure. But with each storm, this nation has gained strength and has grown to become greater in statue to become and remain the greatest nation in the world.

When our forefathers sat down to write the constitution, they started out by proclaiming that this nation shall be a government of the republic of the United States of America and shall be a government of the people. For decades now, the trend of our government has been to take government rule from the people. In many cases, our voting rights have been taken away, and big government made appointments and changes that were previously made through elections. This was one of the first moves our government made toward socialism. Under a socialistic government, there are no voting rights, and other individual freedoms are taken away from the people. In most cases, countries under socialism are controlled and run by a dictator who creates and dictates complete control over the people. During a recent campaign, President Trump, the forty-fifth president of the United States, referred to America's big government as a form of socialism. Actually, he called this form of government "the swamp." And in his first campaign, he vowed to change our swamp government back to the people's rule. A big war is currently going on in our country and part of it is caused by the changes being made in the "swamp," under his first term. In the first part of this book, I list some of these changes on how some of them are being made by localizing and not socializing our government.

Four Hundred Years of Greatness

It has been almost four hundred years since our forefathers landed and took anchor at Plymouth Rock, and since that time, America has become known as a great nation and is recognized as the leader of all nations. We have managed to hold to those foundations and beliefs that were ratified by a constitution, which started off with a declaration that all men are created equal, and each person is free to worship as he believes. This constitution has helped establish a government that is controlled and operated by the people, for the people, and of the people. This government shall be governed by those who are elected through a voting of the rich, the middle class, and the poor. Under this system, a society of Christians who crossed the ocean in a boat in the early 1600s started what became the greatest nation of many. It has, from the beginning, taken in immigrants from other nations and, even in the past year, has had over one million new immigrants from other nations apply for asylum in the United States.

For several years now, this nation seems to be a divided nation. This has been showing up in many areas. Instead of an enthusiasm and belief in the republic and respect and honor for old glory, there has been a lot of hate replacing the love for our country. Instead of standing and placing their hand over their heart, many are choosing not to stand while the national anthem is being played. There seems to be no love left for each other and even very little respect for one another. If you don't believe, that just get on the freeway and cut in the other driver's lane, no, better not do that because road rage has resulted in hundreds of deaths recently. Very few people still attend church, and most young people are not taken to church by their parents. There are very few that can tell you who Jesus Christ is! Love for our neighbor has turned to hate, and it is, "Get out of my way or I'll knock you out." Prisons are so full that we have to release many of those in prison early to make space for the new ones. America, where is your sting? Has the state and church war grown to something greater? Have we entered into a holy war? Are we being seized by an invasion of an enemy from another nation? You do know that the Muslim bible calls Christians infidels, and the mission is to kill the infidels. The more infidels a Muslim can take out, the higher the position will be in the world of hereafter. Now think about this: There are over thirty-one million Muslims that are citizens in the United States. In fact, have you seen the four new congress women recently who make no bones that they are Muslims? Did you know there is one US city that reports to be of 95 percent Muslim? This city is located in the state of Michigan. They have even put a sign up that tell visitors visiting that city, if you are not a Muslim, do not plan to stay in this city. Christians, it is time for us to rumble! If you are too old to rumble, then at least get out and vote.

Where are the Christians? It's Sunday; why are they not in church? Have they quit attending church? Where are their kids? How can we stand by and let big government take God out of our society? Why have they taken God completely out of our public schools? What happened to the last commandment Christ gave to us to love one another? How can we return the government to the people? Is Christ still the truth, the life, and the way? Who said we are no longer a Christian nation?

We've got a lot to do, but we still haven't found the Christians. We sent for the media to round them up so they can rumble with us. We put it on TV, radio, in the newspaper. Or did we?

Come to think of it; I never saw it on any recent news releases. The media did tell Christians not to worry about getting out to vote because elections were already decided, and their vote would not matter. If we vote for fig government, will we, the people, keep our voting rights? Where have the Christians gone? Why have they quit attending church? How long can we stand by and allow 15 percent to take God out of our life and, most especially, out of the schooling and the training up of our children? Our forefathers founded this nation as a nation under God, conceived in liberty, justice, and the pursuit of happiness. Christ gave us a new commandment that we should love one another. We are failing on all accounts.

It is sad that the church seems to have no direction. If only the church had a donkey, maybe God could use the donkey to talk to us. There is a story in the Bible, found in Numbers 22:28, where God spoke through a donkey to talk to one of His prophets. The story tells of a prophet who was going against what God had told him to do, and God had to use a donkey to tell the prophet to think through what he was about to do. Wouldn't it be great if the church could find us donkey to talk to us? Then we could have our ass talk to us. Have you ever had your ass talk to you? Maybe this book will stir your thinking and motivate you back to enjoying the land of milk and honey. It might happen if you will put it in gear and get out to vote.

A WORD FOR YOU WHO DON'T BELIEVE IN GOD

Is there a god, or is God dead as some claim? Why does it matter?

In the 1960s, there was an influx of immigrates who did not believe in the same God that our forefathers worshipped. There were protests by many about the open prayer in public schools. To be fair to those who did not worship alike, schools ruled to remove all prayer in schools.

If we fast-forwarded to 2020 from the 1960s, today, almost everything pertaining to God has been removed from our public schools. When our forefathers first opened public schools, it was common to teach the Bible. In fact, up to just several years back, classes based on the Bible were offered as an elective class in high schools. Today, there are lawsuits filed against school districts to remove God and anything relating to God completely from our public schools. Some twenty years ago, one of our TV networks ran an open survey about taking the words "in God we trust" from our currency. According to the network, this survey proved to be the largest response the network had ever had to a survey. They basically asked the question for callers to give their opinion on keeping "in God we trust" on our coins and bills. The survey polled over 85 percent of the callers who wanted to keep the words on our money. At that time, it seems, from this and other surveys, that there were still some 85 percent of Americans who still believed in God. I have often wondered lately with the influx of immigrants what that count would be today?

What caused this turnaround that seems to take God out of our society? I'll give you a couple of my thoughts. My first question is, why do we have to adapt our government to adhere to changing our rules to fit the laws of those who immigrate to America?

Why should we change our way of praying just because this is different from the way those who have immigrated to this country pray? Why did they choose to come to America? Was it to convert America to conform to their beliefs and way of life? Why should America change to fit their way of life? If you have become a citizen of the United States of America, realize that you should be the one to adapt to America's way of life. After all, America has opened its doors to you. Relax, join with us, and enjoy being a part of the greatest nation known as the United States of America, land of the free.

There was a time when America was thriving on freedom. Our forefathers had established a nation under God that was thriving on love and care for each other. As an answer to understand why all the changes were being made, a national television station decided to conduct the survey mentioned above, and 85 percent voted to keep the "in God we trust" on our currency. With 85 percent responding, that meant that 85 percent voted not to change the "in God we trust" probably were Christians.

Recently, the courts ordered the *Ten Commandments* be removed from all government facilities. As a result, even though a vast majority of Americans call for the commandments to remain in place, the government not only removed the commandments but directed that schools no longer could quote the commandments in public schools. Have you ever read the Ten Commandments? It says love your neighbor, don't steal, don't lie (or hear false witness against your neighbor), and don't commit adultery. Almost everything that is commanded in them is just a repeat of our basic laws.

For over a decade, there has been an effort to remove everything pertaining to God. It seems to have started in the 1960s when a court order was enforced to remove all prayer from our public schools.

This has been an all-out effort to divide America, and there seems to be an all-out attack on the godly principles that our forefathers worked so hard to put into the founding of this great country.

It seems to have started when our churches fell into the "last days" scripture that the apostle Paul wrote: "In the last days... people will have a form of godliness, hut deny the power of God" (NLT). All of sudden, our Spirit-filled churches began to lose attendance and a great falling away of those who believed that the Bible was God's Word to the people, and it was God's way of talking to His people.

There seemed to be a movement away from God, reaching all the way to the supreme court of the United States. They began to give out rulings that were in conflict with God's Word, and many of these rulings sccmcd to divide the principles our country was founded on. Many of these rulings, instead of lining up with the constitution, were in conflict with the Bible and the constitution of the United States. Instead of uniting the States of the United States of America, many of these rulings seemed to divide the states.

A push to divide this nation has grown to the point that our nation is once again in a civil war similar to the Civil War that was fought in the 1860s. Remember! When brother against brother and child against father became so common, it divided not only the country but families. The war we are involved in nowadays has not resulted in a *blood war* but has caused love and brotherly love to become almost void in this nation. Hate has replaced love.

No longer will marriage be limited to man and woman, but the courts have now condoned that it is legally okay for a man to marry a man and/or a woman to marry another woman. Openly, it became common for relationships to be man with man and for women to be involved with other women. This has become so common that several of the states have announced they accept and recognize same-sex marriage. When God made man, He created both male and female, and at the same time, He sanctioned marriage as a union between man and woman. He blessed them and told them to multi-ply and replenish the earth and subdue it. Then when God saw that (as recorded in the first chapter of Romans in the Living translation of the Bible) "the women turned against the natural way to have sex and instead indulged in sex with each other, and the men, instead of having normal sexual relationships with women, burned with lust for each other and did shameful things with other men." It goes on to say that God abandoned them to their shameful desires. In the original King James version, it says that God turned them over to a reprobate mind. In the thirty-second verse of chapter 1 of Romans, God said that those who live this kind of life should be aware that this is a sin unto death. Those who wonder about life after death should at least be aware that God said those who continue to commit these acts should be aware that this is a sin unto death.

This book points out that our nation is no longer a three-class country but is almost in the final stages of becoming a two-class nation: the rich and the poor. This is being displayed by our approach to health care. In America, the rich must pay big bucks to obtain health insurance coverage, and those who can't afford the high cost of insurance can apply to the government for assistance through the federal government.

In fact, a recent ruling by the supreme court has authorized that federal taxes can now be used to pay the premiums on insurance policies for low-income families. Instead of providing health coverage to low-income families, the government could supplement payments to insurance companies to cover their high cost of health care premiums. At the same time, the insurance companies have increased health care cost to those in the higher income brackets. What really broke the camel's back, anyone who chose not to buy health insurance (called Affordable Health Care Act) was subject to an extra income tax penalty for not buying insurance coverage for health care. It became increasingly hard to tell if the government works for the insurance companies or the insurance companies work for the government. Either way, neither seems to be working, and new legislation was recently passed that declared this tax was unconstitutional. At this time, our health care in America is all "up in the air."

Oh, church, where is your sting? It may be time for the church to rumble!

In this book, we are calling on our churches to help return our country back to *one nation under God.*

Bottom Line: How Do We Win the Holy War?

We must find a way to return America and Americans back to seeking first the kingdom of God." The Scripture says to "seek first the kingdom of God...and all these things will be added unto you." Maybe we should make the first step and *go back to church* and return government back to a government *of the people, by the people, and for the people.*

Why not take the scripture quoted on the cover of this book, adapt it to heart, and do what God told Israel on how he would heal their land?

It is time to once again read the Scripture from the Living Bible translation, 2 Chronicles 7:14. Remember this: "Then if those who are called by my name will humble themselves and pray and seek my face and turn from their wicked ways. I will hear from heaven and will forgive their sins and heal their land." It also said in verse 15 (this is God talking): "I will listen to every prayer made in my place" (He is referring to the house of God or church). But do yourself a favor and do it, don't just read it. Just reading it is not enough to heal our land; we have to bring this nation back to God.

A War between
Church and State!

Locauze, don't socialize, our government

Never before has this nation been more divided than it is today. Even when our nation had become divided by a moral force that developed when a large part of this country had forgotten or chose to ignore the basic theme of our constitution, God created all men equal. Big government seems to have taken half of this nation from God, and many of them have made money their God. There is a scripture in God's Word in Matthew 6:24. That reads like this: "No man can serve two masters. For you will hate one and love the other or be devoted to one and despise the other. *You cannot serve both God and money*" (NLT).

A divided house cannot stand

Can a brother get a two-dollar flop? Not many of you will have a clue what I am talking about. This is a term commonly used in a popular poker game called Texas hold 'em. This is a game where each person is dealt two cards and then there is a basic bet before another three cards are turned up to match the holder's cards. The minimum *bet is two dollars and can be more. To nongamblers, anything above two dollars becomes gambling, since you have no way of determining if your cards will match the* next three turned up. If you can get by with a two-dollar bet before the next three cards are turned up, you can know if you want to continue to play or get out without losing a lot of money.

In a roundabout way, you could compare life in America to the game of Texas hold 'em. When our forefathers founded this country, they all desired to see a "two-dollar flop." I guess another way of saying it is they tried to keep things simple. They must have been the first to enact the KISS system. That is, "keep it simple, stupid." They knew very well the cliché, "up in the morning, out on the job, work like the devil for your pay, but that lucky old sun has nothing to do but roll around heaven all day." With the computer age here, not many in America have any understanding about making your living by working the ground for your food. We have cultivated a generation who thinks things we eat are manufactured and have no concept where corn comes from. History is no longer taught, and very few of our children have any knowledge of how this great nation became a great nation. All they know about God is that they have heard that they are odd balls to believe in God. "God bless America" is something only a radical Christian would say. They see the words "in God we trust" on our money and wonder why it is on our money. There probably is not one in a hundred who can quote the Pledge of Allegiance, and the number is even less for those who know the words to The Star-Spangled Banner. They know George Washington's picture is on the dollar bill, but couldn't tell you who he is. They know that there are two major parties, Republican and Democrat, but what each party stands for, they don't have a clue. Even worse, they don't even care.

What is sadder is that half the people in America are estimated to be under age thirty. However, if you attend any church, community, or government meeting, you will be lucky to find anyone under the age of thirty in attendance. But if you want to find someone to protest something, you can easily find a lot of those under age thirty to join in. America, where are we headed?

How can we expect our nation to survive without finding a way to encourage our young people to become a part of this country? Why would they want to take part in government affairs when all they find or hear is a government that is totally divided? All they have to do is lend an ear to what is happening in our congress to quickly make a decision to stay away. Some of them have exposed themselves to quotes like "A divided house cannot stand," or "Be careful not to talk about or refer to God, or you could be put in jail." America is portrayed as a nation that doesn't believe in God and has chosen to ignore that our forefathers founded this country with fundamental beliefs as a nation under God, with liberty and justice for all. *America, America, God, shed His grace on thee, and crown thy good with brotherhood, from sea to shining sea!*

What is happening in America? It might be time to reinstate some of the principles our forefathers installed when they put this nation into being. It might be time for us to wipe the dust off our Bibles and find a way to recognize that there is a God, and He is a God of love and somehow regain not only respect for Him but our leaders, neighbors, and fellowman. Take out the Bible and adhere to those commandments in it. One is that we once again love our neighbor. If we could pinpoint one thing that our forefathers had going for them, it was that they had a love, or you might feel more comfortable in saying they cared one for another. Our constitution so adequately outlines that this nation is a nation of the people, for the people, and by the people, but that doesn't seem to reflect where we are today. From the top down, America has become a nation that has learned to rip apart our president, official representatives, and community leaders right on down to our neighbors. Even worse, families are no longer together, and it is not unusual for children to leave home and never to speak to their parents again. This lack of love for one another has created a sense of apathy that has developed into a depth of unforgiveness that is destroying our families, communities, and faith.

Whether you are a Christian, a Jew, or any other faith, you have to agree that the people in this great country need to get back to caring for one another. If you think about it, our schools, our health care, and our life in general would be better if we could love and respect others as much as we love ourselves. If a person needs help, don't call on your neighbor because he can't afford to get involved. That seems to be the attitude of most Americans. If those great Americans who penned our constitution could come back in an effort to fix the problems that our nation faces today, I have no doubt that the first thing they would say to us is that we rekindle respect and love for each other and allow this love to extend to a love and respect once again for our country. Before it is too late, find a way to put the theme America was built on back into our lives: "Together we stand, divided we fall!"

IS GOD DEAD?

It hasn't been too long ago that there was a movement in this country that was founded on the idea that God was dead. This movement emphasized that this God our forefathers believed in was now dead. I will never forget when I was driving with my son who at that time was only a teenager, and he had heard of this movement and said to me, "Dad, how can anyone believe that God is dead?" He then pointed out the window, and he said to me to look and see the beauty of creation. It happened to be the time of year when all the colors were coming out, and he was right. I looked out and saw a beauty that only God could have created.

Needless to say, this movement didn't last very long. But right on its heels was an even more destructive move to declare that God did not exist. They began to take prayer out of our schools; they went about claiming that anyone who believed in God was misled. Worse yet, they began to push our government to remove God and the very mention of God and vowed to punish anyone who mentioned God. This movement reflected that our forefathers were a bunch of fanatics, and the whole idea they instilled in this country should be changed. They insisted that the Ten Commandments should be removed from all public facilities. They pushed to legalize abortion and insisted that God, or any reference to Him, be eliminated from all government functions. You know what, it is sad to say they succeeded. Lawsuits were filed to take God out of our pledge, and Christmas was no longer Christmas. In place of saying Merry Christmas, it became Happy Holidays. As a result, this nation that was established as one nation under God (because of a few people) became a nation that began to ignore God. That nation that once evolved around the favor of God had become a nation that received fewer and fewer of the blessings from God. This movement is still active and has a goal to make America an atheist nation.

It is imperative that we find a way to repair some of the malfunctions taking place in America. First of all, we must immediately reevaluate our educational system. America is spending more money than ever educating our children, and we are still graduating young people from high school who cannot read or write. We must put reading, writing, and arithmetic back into our school system and bring our schools back to basics. Somehow, we have to put parents back into the picture and once again emphasize home training. Revert to a simple program, especially during our children's younger years. Allow our children space to grow up and experience the normal growth periods that God intended. Babies can't eat steaks; children can't drive cars (or shouldn't be operating computers); teenagers should be involved in learning process to become adults, and college should be a place where our young people go to become businesspeople, not alcoholics. I recently visited a businessman who related to me that it was almost impossible to employ anyone who was willing to work. No wonder businessmen are looking for immigrants to work. Unlike our forefathers who taught their children to give an honest day's work, we have educated a society that wants to start employment at an executive level.

Next, we have to work on our health care system to make it become more affordable and find a way that all people are created equal (health care wise). We need to make health care available to every person and keep the cost down so no one will wind up in the poor house just because of a serious illness. Families should not be forced to make a decision to feed their family or purchase family health insurance. Our governmental system is a great element in our nation; however, if we allow the government to provide all things to all people, then the right of individual freedom will go by the wayside. It just might be time that we revert to a government of the people, by the people, and for the people. A good start toward this would be to bring the basic operation back to a community level.

Somehow, we have to bring everything back to a majority rule. America has operated too long, and we have been too complaisant in allowing a minority to rule, thus allowing laws and rules to be enacted, which limit an individual's freedom. It is sad that a few (according to the surveys that revealed 15 percent of the populace) make all the rules and regulations. Just as an example, the majority of people feel that abortion is wrong, yet we have a law that makes it legal. Also, did you know that a new law allows schools (even elementary level) to pass out birth control to our kids without the parents knowing it? The working mom is here to stay, and we must find a way to pass on family heritage to our children even if they are being trained through day cares and schools from birth on.

Finally, it is time to reinstate the church back into our communities. Instill God and God's love once again to a new level. Teach our children about our heritage, and teach our children about the great men who founded this wonderful nation based on a trust in God. Reactivate a voting system that will elect God-fearing people to our White House and congress. We must formulate a system to make sure that we appoint judges who can make right judgments that adhere to the constitution. Somehow, we have to bring this nation back to a government of the people, by the people, and for the people. Instead of removing the Ten Commandments from our government, we need to renew them and once again become a godly nation. In the Bible, God instructed Moses to encourage the people to teach the commandments to their children. The Israelites were further instructed to talk about them when they sit at home, when they were walking, when they lay down, and when they first awakened. The Bible goes on to command the people to write them on their hands and to write them on the post of their houses and on their gates. No doubt, this was what inspired our forefathers to carve these commandments on our courthouses and public buildings. *Awake, awake, America. Put off your slumber. Rise up and take control.*

At times it is important to turn the other cheek, but there is a time to stand up for right. If it isn't that time now, I am afraid it will never be the right time. God is not dead, and we should stand up to those who want to take him out of everything America stands for. Again, to quote Scripture: "To everything, there is a season and a time to every purpose under the heaven, a time to be born, and a time to die, a time to plant and a time to pluck up that which has been planted. There is a time to heal, a time to break down, and a time to build up." It goes on to say, "There is a time to weep and time to laugh, a time to mourn and a time to dance. There is a time to cast away stones, a time to gather stones together, a time to embrace, and a time to refrain from embracing. There is a time to receive, a time to lose, a time to keep, and a time to cast away. There is a time to rend, a time to sew, a time to keep silent, and a time to speak. Then it goes on to say that there is a time to love, a time to hate, a time of war, and a time of peace."

In studying the history and the founding of this great nation, it is quite evident that our forefathers founded this county using the Bible as a guide. No doubt, they found the scripture that outlines that there are three things that will endure. These are faith, hope, and love, with love being the greatest of these. Faith represents a belief in God. Hope is a desire to anticipate a confident expectation, and love is a commandment given to us by God. These three things seem to come to life when great stress is placed on this country. Things like war, depression, hurricanes, earthquakes, floods, fires, and other things of destruction. Every time one of these disasters rocks this nation, all three of these traits (faith, hope, and love) arise to help bring us through the storms of life. We once again become a nation of the people, by the people, and for the people. But how long can this nation endure if we continue to remove faith, hope, and love from our country? Look at our school system and what has happened to it since we removed God. Look at our government and how divided it has become since God is no longer reverenced in it. Look at our welfare system and how it is failing since we took caring for the poor and needy away from the church. Same thing has occurred with our health care system and with recent health care legislation we are working on, turning it over to big government. It won't work because it takes personal care and love out. We could go on and on, but it boils down to putting God back into our nation instead of taking Him out. Maybe Billy Graham's daughter was right, "maybe God is fed up with us trying to take Him out of our lives, and He has decided to get out of our lives." If there is still 85 percent of

Americans who believe in God, why don't we wake up and smell the roses and take a stand before it is too late. There are too many people in America who do not have a clue about what they believe or don't believe. *You have to stand for something, or you will fall for anything.*

WHAT HAPPENED TO GOD BLESS AMERICA?

For nearly four hundred years now, God has continued to bless America. From the start, the favor of God flowed out to America. In fact, even before the pilgrims landed on the shores of America, God was reverenced as being the power that brought these pilgrims across the ocean in a makeshift boat. Recognizing that God's direction was important in forming a new nation, the first thing these Pilgrims did was to offer a time of Thanksgiving to this God. For those of you who were never taught this, this first thanksgiving was the beginning of what is now the Holiday we observe as Thanksgiving. God responded by sending some of the natives co befriend the pilgrims and dine with them. I have to believe this was part of the Favor of God and was God's way of saying that He was pleased to bless them. If you will study history, you will find that from that time on our forefathers instilled God in every element of their venture. When it came to the writing of the Constitution, they selected ministers and those well embedded in God and the things of God to write this Constitution. As a result, this nation became a nation under God.

Now, there are those few in this country working overtime to assure that America no longer honors God or the things of God. They started by taking prayer out of our schools; they proceeded to remove anything pertaining to God from our society. If we continue on the same course, it should only be a matter of time when we will have to take God and worship of God underground. Freedom of religion is already being challenged, and this nation under God is currently found in court to eliminate the mere mention or referral of God. So far, we have been able to retain the "in God we trust" on our money. But given time, you can rest assured that these minority groups will direct their efforts toward removing this.

The first question we must ask ourselves is why we have become so apathetic that we, the majority, are sitting back and allowing this to happen to our nation.

Up to this point, about all we have determined is that America has a problem. If we could boil it down to one major thing, we would have to agree that not one but many things have contributed to a downward trend. Whether you believe the story of Balaam and how the donkey talked to him or not, you will have to admit that America could be better served if we were all riding on a donkey that had the ability to tell us to change directions. I know we have invented computerized things that instruct us when to turn right or left, but we need to cultivate a belief that evolves to a *trust* in God. Instead of following a few who are working hard to convince Americans to ignore God, we must stand up and reevaluate where we are heading, and once again return our nation to one nation under God, indivisible with liberty and justice for all."

When America was first founded, it was a nation that encompassed a three-class system. This system included the poor, the middle class, and the rich. It first started with the majority of the people considered in the middle class. Even when large numbers of immigrants began to migrate to this country, this nation allowed these immigrants to become a part of the middle class. They were allowed to own their own businesses, vote, and express their beliefs, and they were allowed to worship as they pleased. Most of the laws that governed this society were designed to include this middle-class people. Even down to taxation, this class paid the most toward operating the community and government. This group seemed to have a vent toward trusting in God and most recognized that God was in control of this nation. They had no problem in God being included in schooling of their children. They had no problem placing their hand on the Bible and swearing in court. And when Christmas came around, they all greeted each other with "Merry Christmas." The 10 percent that didn't go to church were included in the prayers of the other 90 percent that attended church. If a neighbor needed a cup of sugar, they could go to the next-door neighbor and borrow a cup. They learned that many of the highlights of life were times they got together and fellowshipped with each other. They kept all things at a simple level. And when one in the community suffered a loss or illness, the entire community got together and met the need. They discovered, and put into practice the scripture that it is more blessed to give than it is to receive.

Even when this nation endured a brother-against-brother civil war, they were able to overcome this hurt and rejoin together. As a result, this nation became an even greater nation than before. The same thing happened when the great depression engulfed this country. Then came the test of tests when another country willfully attacked this nation. Again, the response was an act of together-ness that surpassed everything else. God was recognized as one that America could place their full trust in. This nation not only survived but also became a nation that prevailed as a great nation under God, with liberty and justice for all. Since that war, this nation has sur-vived devastating earthquakes, hurricanes, fires, and disasters, and with each has found that God is not dead, and most Americans were able to recognize that God is still blessing America.

With the rapid pace and technology in the past twenty-five years, this nation seems to have moved from being a three-class sys-tem. There are very few middle-class people left in this country. Those that are poor seem to get poorer, and the rich get richer. Majority no longer rules. And even though surveys reflect that 85 percent still believe in God, there is very little trust in God remaining in America.

Many blame the government. Many say it is immigration. Others relate it to apathy. Still others blame the church, and we could go on and on. Our government is not doing its job. Our education programs are not working. Our health care has taken a dump. Our children are not being taught that there is a God, and our colleges are turning out more drunks than doctors. Our voting system is dis-torted, and there is no longer a respect or reverence toward our pres-ident or elected officials. We once were a nation respected by other nations, but now we have become a nation that is hated by other nations. Once known as a country that was self-sufficient, we have become a nation with dependence on other nations for subsistence. Our belief in God—or maybe I should say, our trust in God—no longer is part of life in America.

So far, we have only talked about acute problems facing this nation. We haven't even talked about why these problems exist and what caused this great country to develop into such a state of being. We have stated that we need to find a means of correcting some of the most acute of these things in order to survive. But before we can attempt to solve any of these problems, we need to define a base root. It is time to realize that we cannot expect a return of God's blessings to America until we get back to the basics upon which this nation was founded. We are going to have to carry the majority rule and belief that there is a God and turn that belief into a trust in God. We need to dust the dust off our Bibles. And instead of allowing a minority to dictate and destroy our principles, take out our bill of rights and crush the enemy. In the book of Proverbs, the Scripture outlines a direct course that would behoove all Americans to adhere to. This is especially true since we don't have a donkey, like Balaam had, to direct us. This scripture is, "Trust in the Lord with all your heart and lean not to your own understanding, in all your ways acknowledge Him and He shall direct your paths" (KJV). If you believe in God, try trusting in God; it might help turn our country around. We are at war, whether you know it or not. *Remember 9/11!*

LIKE IT OR NOT, WE ARE AT WAR!

If we could bring back President Lincoln and ask him to deliver a speech to Americans, it might go like this:

> "Some 240 years ago, our forefathers penned and signed, one of the greatest documents ever produced since the Bible. This writing was the constitution of the United States of America. For over three hundred years, this constitution has stood the test and, like America, has proved to be above all others."
>
> "Now this constitution is being tested from every level, and the idea of our trust in God is being challenged from all angles. It has now reached a point that this nation that was established as one nation under God is being called to question and that government of the people is no longer by the people and for the people. We are now engaged in a civil war very similar to that Civil War we were involved in when I delivered the Gettysburg Address. True, we haven't reached the bloodshed that took place in the first Civil War, but each civil war was brought about because of moral beliefs.
>
> "The first war was to correct a moral dilemma that had gripped our nation about slavery. The war we are now engaged in is a war

between church and state. The conflict revolves around whether there is a God and should the state recognize that this country should continue to reverence God. Those forefathers who together founded this nation had no idea that this government would find itself at war with the church, especially when every one of them had a devout belief in God. Like the previous civil war, this nation is once again being tested to see if a nation under God can continue to endure. It is proper that all men be afforded a voice in the basic operation of this country, but to remove God or any reference to God from our constitution would be against the majority rule and would violate the very principle upon which this nation was founded. We have stood the tests for all these years—enduring famine, wars, and massive destructions—all under the name of God. Now we must once again stand up for our rights. We don't need another 9/11 or any other form of terrorism. We must not only keep God foremost in our society but reinstate into our culture a trust in God and regain a love for our country, our neighbors, and ourselves. Recognize that this war between church and state is only a rebellion against God with a goal to destroy this great nation. It is time for us to rise up, and take a stand, and take back control of our country. To quote John F. Kennedy, "Ask not what your country can do for you, but ask what you can do for your country." Dust off your Bibles, get back into church, and let's win this war."

Of course we know that it is impossible to bring "Abe" Lincoln back, and this is a fictitious speech. But if you read it carefully, you might pick up a lot of truth in it. One thing for sure is we are knee-deep in a war between church and state. If 85 percent of us still believe in God, it is time to dust off our Bibles and start listening to that inner spirit that God has placed in each of us. Draw from the Bible just as our forefathers did when they wrote the constitution. To quote one scripture: "Seek first the kingdom of God" (KJV).

But before you can seek first the kingdom of God, you must understand what the kingdom of God is. Many who profess a belief in God don't even understand what the kingdom of God is. This is especially true when the Scripture tells us that the kingdom of God is within us. This tells me that God lives within us. And when the Bible refers to the kingdom of God, it is not talking about the kingdom of heaven. This may be why many have such a hard time trying to live up to man's standards of never sinning. We are all sinners, saved by grace. And if we believe the Bible and John 3:16, we can live as Christians and enjoy abundant life. No doubt, this explains the kingdom of God being in us. It also explains why the Bible states that we have a spiritual body living in a physical body, and we are set apart from all other living creatures because "God breathed into us and made us a living soul." Let me give you a little more insight into this according to the Bible.

Before we go into detail about this, let's review how God made us in His image and how the Bible, from the creation of man, relates how God has dealt with man as a Triune being (spirit, body, and soul). A good example of this is displayed by the story of the donkey talking to a prophet. No doubt, God had to find a way to communicate with man, especially since God had made man a free-willed individual. Understand that, in modem-day terms, man is his own boss.

Before I go any further, I have to assume that since 85 percent of you believe in God that you also believe that God created man and that He is the Supreme Being over all things. In providing a means of forgiveness when we go against God, He sent His Son who died on the cross to redeem us from our sins. And if we believe, He will send His Holy Spirit to dwell in our spirit. If you have a basic belief that the Bible is true and is the inspired Word of God, and you accept Jesus as your Savior, you not only are guided by God's Spirit but, according to John 3:16, you can have eternal life. Added to this, as an American, you join with those who wrote the constitution toward a trust in God.

How do we know right from wrong? God has built into man (God breathed into man and made him a living soul) a measure of faith that gives man a means of direct contact with God. Some believe that this soul is our conscience. In a way, I agree with this mainly because I have never heard of a person's conscience giving bad advice. However, I think it goes a little further than just making us aware of right or wrong. According to the Bible, the soul is the director of our being. Let me explain it like this: We have been talking about how our country is involved in a civil war between church and state. There is also another war going on, and this is a war between our physical and spiritual beings. The Bible outlines to us that the soul is the part of us (that third part of our being) that directs our actions and encompasses our emotions, directs our decisions, and our will. This soul is considered by many to be the mind of our spirit. The soul is also the battleground of the war between our physical (flesh) and our spiritual (which is where the spirit of God resides. Remember, "the kingdom of God is within you"). Since the soul is the part of you that directs your being, it becomes the battleground where the spirit (good) is fighting against the physical or flesh (bad) with each vying for control of the soul. The Bible puts it like this: "For the flesh lusts against the Spirit and the Spirit is in contrast against the flesh: and these are contrary the one to the other so that you cannot do the things that you would" (KJV).

The Bible goes on to say that "the 'works' of the flesh are manifested through sexual immorality, impure thoughts, eagerness for lustful pleasure, idolatry, participation in demonic activities, hostility, quarreling, jealousy, outbursts of anger, selfish ambition, divisions, the feeling that everyone is wrong except those in your own little group, envy, drunkenness, wild parties, and other kinds of sin." Then the Scripture tells us that anyone living this sort of life will not inherit the kingdom of God. Now I'm not the judge, but it does say kingdom of God, not kingdom of heaven.

On the other side, when the Holy Spirit controls our lives, we will produce this kind of fruit: love, joy, peace, patience, kindness, goodness, faithfulness, gentleness, and self-control.

My question to you is, What side of the war are you on, and have you undergone training, and have you passed the test to enter the war? From the time of creation, God has required man to make choices. Understand, God created man to have someone to love Him. It is a lot like a father wants his children to love him. Up to this time, God had the angels. However, they were pledged to God and, even though they were able to go against God, they had no means of redemption. There is a story in the Bible about an angel (he is sometimes referred to as the fallen angel) who chose to go against God. And because of his perversion and plotting in defiance of God, he was kicked out of heaven along with a third of the angels. If you are up-to-date on your Bible, you will also know that this angel is now referred to as Satan in the Bible. The other third of the angels that were kicked out are demons.

Now that you have had your Bible lesson, let's get back to why man was made. God created man and breathed into him a living soul with a free will. Since man was made in the image of God, God realized that man would also need someone to love him, so he took a part of man and made woman. Just a little side note, I am so glad God made woman, and he allowed me to spend forty-five years with a beautiful, loving woman who was not only my helpmate in life, mother of my children, but a faithful companion.

After creating man and woman, God placed them in what the Bible describes as an all-inclusive garden called Eden. He gave man dominion over this garden and everything in it. However, God placed in the garden a tree and instructed the man and woman not to eat the fruit from this tree. I'm sure this was all in God's plan to enact man's free will. The woman chose to disobey God and ate the forbidden fruit and gave it to the man, and he ate it also. This act caused all future men to be born into the world as sinners. My point is that man became a free-willed being, and you are free to choose to love God or to reject Him.

There are stories throughout the Bible where God instructs His servants to challenge the people to choose whom they will serve. One such story is recorded when God told the people to put away all other gods and serve Him only. Joshua, who was a man God had appointed to lead His people, stood up and spoke to the people that as for him and his family, they would serve the Lord.

America has reached a place that we, as Americans, are going to have to make a choice whether we are in the army of the church or the state. If the survey is true that 85 percent of Americans still believe in God, it shouldn't be much of a war. However, I am sure that many of those who responded to the surveys had no intentions of making a choice to serve God. It is a good chance that most of those only agreed to claiming God, and chances are, the majority of them couldn't even begin to explain to you why "in God we trust" is found on all our money.

Let's analyze just what the 85 percent figure means. First of all, it was just recently announced that the population in America has now elevated to over 300,000,000 people. If we took 85 percent of this, then we would come up with some 250,000,000 people considered as Americans that still believe in God. Next question, if we were putting an army together, how many of this 250 million would be eligible to fight in this war? I read the other day that nearly one-half of the people in America are believed to be under the age of thirty. If that is true, then only those eighteen and above could participate in the war. Let's round the numbers off. That would leave 120,000,000. There are over 2,000,000 incarcerated. That eliminates 1,700,000 (85 percent of 2,000,000). We are now down to 118,000,000. Since this will be a volunteer force, then we could easily take out another 18,000,000 people. We are now down to 100,000,000 considered to be a part of the church side. One consolation is that the 15 percent that expressed not to believe in God had to be broken down in the same manner.

One hundred million is still a good-size army. After all, drawing from the past, when our forefathers wrote the constitution, there probably wasn't even a million people considered as residents of this country.

There is a story in the Bible about a young man God called to gather up an army to fight God's enemy. If you will allow me, I would like to offer my thoughts on how this story could give some direction to America and how the battle can be won if we could learn to put more trust in God. The story shows how God used a small army to defeat a huge army without a physical battle. That tells me that we may not need 100,000,000 to win the war. Maybe if we could get a fourth, or 25,000,000, of those who say they believe in God to get sincere enough in their belief in God to trust in God, then God will do the rest. The story in the Bible was no doubt another one of those stories that our forefathers drew from when they founded this great nation. They were very careful to instill God and things of God into everyday life in an effort to avoid losing the favor of God.

This is the story of a young man named Gideon. Gideon was a member of the Israelite nation and a member of one of the weakest clans in that nation. The Israelites had experienced peace in their land for forty years. However, they had forgotten and ignored God. (This could be compared to the present state of being where America is today.) As a result, God allowed the Midianites, who were very cruel, to gain control of the Israelites for seven years. Things continued to get worse. And when the Israelites planted crops, the Midianites would destroy their crops, and the Israelites had nothing to eat. Israel was reduced to starvation, and their land had been stripped bare.

No doubt, our forefathers read this story and were careful to instruct the people of this nation to keep God foremost in their minds. They seemed to know that without the favor of God, this nation couldn't stand. This just might be why they insisted on putting God into all aspects of this country. They printed the words "in God we trust" on our money; they put God in our pledge and even carved the Ten Commandments on our courthouses and public buildings. They took to heart how God told Moses to instruct the people to talk about these commandments and of God to each other, "post them on their houses, on their gate posts, and etc." Now we are in a battle that seems to be working hard to take God out. Whether you believe in God or not, be aware that if we take God out, we take the blessings of God out. Then the crops quit growing, earthquakes come, storms, floods, and fire cause devastation, and instead of the land of the free, we become a captive land.

Finally, the Israelites had enough and began to review how their forefathers had trusted in God when He brought them out of bondage in Egypt. They cried out to the Lord for help. It just might be time for Americans to cry out to God for help; after all, we seem to have many of the same things happening, maybe in a different context, like 9/11, hurricanes, fires, and earthquakes.

When the children of Israel called out to the Lord for help, God sent a prophet who reminded them that God's blessing was lifted from them because they had worshipped other gods and had refused to listen to God. (Wow, how this fits America.) This may be why America is finding the favor of God less and less. Although 85 percent say they still believe in God, we seem to have put other things before Him. One thing for sure is there are very few in America who know how to completely trust in God. The sad thing is we are not teaching trust in God to our children. You have to know that there are other nations vying to control America and would give their lives to destroy this nation. *Remember* 9/11?

God heard their prayers and sent an angel who found Gideon and informed him that the Lord's Spirit was with him and Israel. Gideon's first reaction was, "if the Lord is with us, why has all this happened to us and where are all the miracles our ancestors told us about? Didn't they say the Lord brought us up out of Egypt? But now, the Lord has abandoned us and handed us over to the Midianites" (KJV). Doesn't that fit America? If there is a God, why did God allow Katrina, which was a hurricane that destroyed New Orleans and all the fires and disasters that are taking place in America? We say to each other, where is God? God told Gideon to rise up and go with the strength he had been given by God. God told Gideon that he would destroy the Midianites as if fighting against one man. I know most of you are familiar with the story about Gideon and have read how Gideon put out a fleece to test if it was really God who was telling him to head up the army. If you know the story, Gideon put out a fleece, which in modern day would be about the same thing as a sponge, and asked the Lord to make it wet and the ground around it dry. The first night, Gideon wrung out a whole bowl of water, and the ground around it was dry. Then the next night just the reverse, the fleece was dry and the ground around it was wet. This confirmed to Gideon that it was in fact the Lord calling him to lead the army. Again, this rings so true with Americans. "If God wants me to mow the grass, He will let the mower start!" On with the story.

God told Gideon to go to a spring that was near where the Midianites were camped. Gideon had an army of thirty-two thousand troops, and the Midianites were as "vast as the sands on the sea shore." The Lord said to Gideon, "You have too many warriors with you. If I let all of you fight the Midianites, the Israelites will boast to me that they saved themselves by their own strength." (Americans say, "I can handle this job all by myself." They have ignored the Scripture that quotes: "Trust in the Lord with all you heart and lean not to your own understanding, and in all your ways acknowledge God, and He shall direct your paths.") On with the story, God told Gideon to tell the people who were timid or afraid that they could feel free to go home. Wow, 22,000 of them went home. (Boy, isn't this a picture of Americans. They are afraid to be involved and are more than willing to let someone else do the fighting.) This left only 10,000 to fight an army that was too many to number. Would you believe, God said there are still too many. (Keep in mind, before we started relating this story to you, America had an army that was cut down to 100,000,000 that believed in God.) God told Gideon to take the warriors down to the water and divide them into two groups. They would be divided by the way they drank the water. All those who knelt down and formed their hands to make a cup to drink the water were in one group, and those that lay down and drank the water with their mouths in the water became the other group. Then God instructed Gideon to tell the 9,700 who drank with their mouths in the water, to go home. This left only 300 men and God assured Gideon that these 300 could win the war. (I am sure, if God could find just 1 percent of the 100,000,000 in America who qualified to be in the army of the church that the war between the church and state could be won overwhelmingly by the church.) As it stands now, the army of the state is winning the battle with a lot fewer. Let me finish the story. It demonstrates how neat God caused the battle to be won.

This is the best part of the story. The Midianites were camped in a valley that was surrounded by mountains. God told Gideon to go that night and place three groups of 100 at strategic locations, and he gave each man a ram's horn and a clay jar with a torch in it.

He instructed them to keep their eyes on him and to do as he did. Gideon also had a horn and a jar with a torch in it. Gideon blew the horn and broke the jar, and the others, at the same time, blew their horns and broke their jars and shouted, "A sword for the Lord and for Gideon." This must have created widespread fear because all the different armies in the valley began to rush around in panic and began to fight each other with their swords. Those who were not killed fled to places far away. The Israelites went down and gathered up all the cattle, camels, and spoils that were left intact. *To God be the glory!*

The point America can draw from this story is we must find a way to turn our country around and learn to draw from God instead of pushing Him out of our lives. The Bible tells us, if we will draw close to God, He will draw close to us. Instead of the minority rule, we must get back to a nation "of the people, for the people, and by the people." If you still have a donkey and are riding it, listen to it when it talks. Since most of us don't have a donkey to talk to us, we must activate the kingdom of God within us and allow God to talk to us through our spirit or inner man. Just remember this, it all must start with "love one another." *United we stand, divided we fall.*

I have often wondered if our forefathers knew that one day this nation would be so divided that, instead of making laws that protect the people, they are only concerned about destroying one another. Is there a God? Should we retract all our laws that refer to Him? If we pray to Him, are we wasting our time? Were our forefathers off base when they installed God and things that refer to Him in our constitution and even put "in God we trust" on our money?

It is evident that there is now a division in our nation. You must choose to be a liberal (state) or a conservative (church), and like it or not, we are involved in a cultural war just like the TV commentary stated. It might be true that the largest liberal troops are the news media, and the conservative troops are Christians. It's almost like there are signs being put up each day that say: "Choose this day whom you will serve, church or state?" Remember the story I told you about Joshua whom God had chosen to lead the children of Israel after the death of Moses? Joshua had led the nation for many years, and many of the Israelites began to turn to other gods.

Joshua called the people together and reminded them that they should remember how God took care of Noah and his family through the flood, how He had delivered their forefathers from Egypt, and how He led them to the promised land. Joshua then told the people, "If it seems evil unto you to serve the Lord, then choose you this day who you will serve, whether the gods which your fathers served that were on the other side of the flood or other gods. But as for me and my house, we will serve the Lord." Maybe it is time that our leaders and America's fathers rise up and make a stand that as for them and their families, they will choose to trust in God, just like our forefathers did. America seems to be covered up with a state of apathy and a complacency that they don't seem to stand for anything; and as a result, they wind up falling for anything.

Let me give you a little history about how this nation came into being. The initial formation of this country came about when great suppression was being placed on Christians in England.

DISPENSATIONS OF CREATION AND FAITH

So we will be able to equip our armies. We must first determine what kind of war we are involved in. Is it a religious, cultural, or civil war? The answer is yes. When it first started, it was only a religious war. Then it evolved into a cultural war and now has spread to a civil war. If we don't get a handle on it, it could become a physical war. America, with the exception of the great Civil War this country endured, has fought almost every physical war we were involved in on other lands. Up to 9/11, America had never been attacked on our own land. When the Japanese attacked us at Pearl Harbor, it was against America but was not considered an attack on the home front or a direct hit on North America.

I guess if you wanted to get really technical, you could say we are and have been involved for some time in a cultural warfare. There is a popular radio and TV personality who recently wrote a book on cultural warfare. The part of the war he pointed out was that the news media was deeply involved in this war. I read the book, and he was right on, but I felt he only scratched the surface of those involved. Because I have spent most of my life as a Christian, I would say that religious people have contributed more toward the cultural warfare than any other group. At the same time, we can't ignore those elected officials who have so divided our country.

A determined group of these Christians decided that enough was enough. They put together a makeshift boat and enough supplies and headed for a new life and a new country. They were well embedded in a strong belief in God and had a confirmed faith and trust in God. During their intense journey, they encountered severe storms, unknown navigation, bad weather, and food and water shortages. When they reached the shores of this new country, still intact, even those who had a doubt they would ever make it found a true belief and trust in God. If I let my thoughts explore their actions, I would have to believe that the first thing they did on that cold winter day was get together and have a prayer meeting. We do know that just a few days after their arrival, they were careful to come together and have a "thanksgiving feast."

The first building they built was a church house. This was a place where they could come together and thank and worship God for bringing them through the storm. They also used this building as a community center and, according to historical reports, when they gathered to discuss civil affairs, they started the meeting with a prayer. This carried over to the first congress this nation held in 1777 when they met to install the constitution of the United States. This tradition has prevailed in the nation all these years. Now there seems to be a force that chooses to ignore the very principles this nation was founded on and are calling for the removal of all prayer, allegiance to God, and are demanding that God be removed from everything that has anything to do with this country. What is even more sad is there are more of us who believe that we should keep the "in God we trust" on our currency than there are who don't believe in God.

In a recent survey made by one of our national TV networks, a poll was taken to see how many would like to keep the "in God we trust" on our money with an overwhelming response (85 percent) elected to keep the statement on our money. But the war didn't end there, and the 15 percent just dug in and continued their plight. The war goes on. Stand up, America! There is an old song that our forefathers sang. It goes like this: "Stand up, stand up for Jesus, you soldier of the cross. Lift high His royal banner. It must not suffer loss." Or as I stated earlier, you have to stand for something, or you'll fall for anything.

As Americans, we must understand that, like it or not, our nation was and is patterned around the Bible. The problem we are facing today is that God and the Bible are not being passed on to our future generations. Our children know very little about creation, very little about the Bible, and know even less about why God made man. I often wonder why God gave so much power to man and why God had to use different means to communicate with man. It is a good thing that I am not God because I probably would just go around zapping men out. However, God doesn't do that. But there was a time He did wipe out the entire nation, except for one man and his family. Remember Noah and the flood. Here again, I have often wondered why God has had such a hard time communicating with man. But throughout the Bible, we find God had to use many different means to get through to man. In my study of the Bible, I have determined that when God breathed into man and made him a living soul, God established in man a free will and vowed not to go against man's will. It seems to me that this caused a communication gap, and God had to find a way to get through to man. No doubt, this is why he had to use the donkey to get Balaam's attention.

From the get-go, God has allowed man to exercise his own free will, starting with Adam and Eve. Then right off the bat, Cain, Adam and Eve's son, killed his brother Abel. Even though God had made man in the image of God, and He even put a measure of faith into man's makeup, man consistently chose to go against God. God found Himself having to send rains to cause the earth to be flooded and, as stated before, only one family survived. However, if you read the Bible, the big problem was that the sons of God were taking daughters of man as their wives and wound up having giants. The entire universe was in turmoil. You see, God had no choice. At that time there was no redemption or plan in effect to save man from the law of sowing and reaping.

Have you ever wondered why different species of animals cannot mix breed? Dogs can't breed cats, chickens can't cohabit with turkeys, squirrels can't mate with rats, etc. However, man has made one exception to this rule, and that is to breed a horse to a donkey and make a mule. Since this is an exception to God's rule, there is a unique twist to this union. Mules cannot reproduce their own kind. The only way to make a mule is to breed a horse to a donkey. Many times, we fail to realize the completeness of God's creation. We also fail to realize how much power God gave to man when He made man in God's own image, giving man a freedom of choice and a free will. It could be that is why God has had such a hard time communicating with man.

After man ate the fruit of the tree of knowledge, man began to make excuses to God for his disobedience. Remember when God appeared to Adam in the garden after he had eaten the forbidden fruit and God asked him why he was hiding behind the tree, Adam's response was to blame it on "that woman you gave me." According to the Bible, God put into man a measure of faith that allowed man to relate to God. Being a self-taught scholar of the Bible, I have gathered my own opinions of some stories in the Bible. This is especially true when little detail is given about the story. The accounting of the tree of knowledge could easily be expanded to what kind of tree this was. Many have related it to being an apple tree.

However, I gathered my own thoughts about it, and please keep in mind that this is only my opinion and is not to be accepted as factual. Because we are given very little detail about the tree of knowledge and since, by eating the fruit, Adam and Eve seemed to have become aware of their fleshly being, it could be that *sex* was the forbidden fruit. Now don't go off on a tangent with this and start a new religion. But observing how Adam and Eve hid themselves behind a tree when God approached them, it could be that they had explored their flesh. The Scripture does say they realized they were naked and made clothes out of fig leaves. I also noticed that shortly after that, they had their first child, Cain. Scripture does not say that Adam and Eve had any children prior to this. There are so many things in the Bible that I have tried to find answers for myself. For example, where did Cain get his wife? Was she his sister, or was she from another world? I must be honest with you; I really don't know. But don't get too excited because you don't know either. I have to believe that if God had wanted us to know the details, He would have given more detail. This might be one of those things that God threw out to exercise our faith.

Then just before the flood, the Bible relates that when man began to multiply, the sons of God saw the daughters of men that they were beautiful, and they took them as their wives. First question: Who were the sons of God? A lot of Bible scholars say that they were angels. If that is right, why didn't it say angels instead of sons of God? In another place, when it talks about the hereafter, it refers to the saints being part of the sons of God.

Next question: Could it be that Adam and Eve had children before they partook of the tree of knowledge? Then to go on the Scripture relates that when sons of God took the daughters of men as their wives. They bore children who became giants. Really, there is no way of gaining the answer since we have very little to go on from the Scriptures.

Prior to the flood, it is recorded that man lived for several hundreds of years. In fact, the oldest man that ever lived was Methuselah who, according to the Bible, lived 969 years. Adam lived to be 930 years. With the flood, God changed the number of years a man lives on earth. God seemed to say that He was a little put out with having to strive with man all those years. The Scripture confirms that God decided to limit man's days on earth to 120 years. I have no personal knowledge of a man ever living past 120 years in my lifetime. I did have the privilege of meeting a 106-year-old man. Recent insurance studies have brought the average life expectancy of man to 78 years. There is a scripture in the Psalms that states, "The days of our years are threescore (60) and ten, or a total of 70 years, and if by reason of strength, we are given fourscore (80) years" (KJV). However, the Bible records Abraham lived to be 175 years old.

No doubt, God saw the wickedness of man was so great in the earth that, according to Scripture, His "every imagination of the thoughts of man's heart was only evil, and it grieved God." In fact, God was so grieved that He repented that He had made man. The Lord said, "I will destroy man whom I have created from the face of the earth, along with every beast, and every creeping thing, and the fowls of the air, and He repented that He had made them" (KJV).

However, one man, Noah, did find grace in the eyes of the Lord. The Bible puts it this way, "Noah was a just man and perfect in his generations, and Noah walked with God."

God looked upon the earth and saw nothing but corruption, and all flesh had corrupt ways. That is when God decided to destroy all those who inhabited the earth. However, Noah found favor in the eyes of the Lord, and Noah and his family were saved. After the flood destroyed all living things on earth that were not saved in the *ark*, God made a covenant that He would never again smite every living thing. Thank God! At least we know that America still has a good chance of survival.

I'm sure God had to find a better way of communicating with man than He had prior to the flood. This might be when He added to man's spirit a measure of faith that allowed man to have a built-in thirst for God's love. Again, this is my speculation, but I believe this was when God established a new dispensation of faith to bring about a new level of communication between God and man.

Guess what, God found a great man of faith who seemed to fit what God was looking for to establish a new nation. This man's name was Abram, whose name was later changed to Abraham because God made a covenant with him as the father of many nations. This was the beginning of the nation of Israel, which is the nation that America evolved from. Ever heard of referral to the God of Abraham, Isaac, and Jacob? Man operated under the dispensation of faith until God gave Moses the Ten Commandments, which created a new dispensation. This was the dispensation of the law.

DISPENSATION OF LAW

God had made the commitment that He would not destroy mankind again. However, during the dispensation of faith, He still found man's imagination and thoughts to be evil. Under the dispensation of faith, there were a couple of cities called Sodom and Gomorrah that had become extremely evil, and the Scripture records that everything they did was wicked. They had reached a place that the Bible says God had had enough and turned them over to a reprobate mind. The city had become so perverted that God withdrew His blessing and announced that He was going to destroy these cities. When God told Abraham that He was going to destroy Sodom and Gomorrah, Abraham petitioned God that if he could find fifty innocent people within the cities, would He (God) change His mind and not destroy the city? God agreed. It was impossible to find fifty. Then Abraham tried to find forty, then thirty, then twenty, and ten, and each time, God agreed. But not even ten could be found, so God rained down fire and burning sulfur from heaven and destroyed Sodom and Gomorrah. When I recently read this story, my thoughts turned to America and how we are involved in a war between church and state and how this nation is having such a hard time *trusting in God*. We have become a nation that has ignored God and has become so perverted it would make Sodom and Gomorrah look good.

No doubt, this was why God had to make up physical laws for man to combine with the measure of faith just to communicate with man. Let's call this the dispensation of law.

Before we go into the dispensation of the law, let's take a time out and let me explain to you that these are *my* own thoughts, and I have no actual scriptures to repute or confirm this as fact.

Now there have been lots of theologians who have theorized similar dispensations, but none have facts to back them up.

In my opinion, there are basically four periods that God used to mold man toward salvation.

If I were to break them down for you, I would have to say that these dispensations are creation, faith, law, and grace. I have already reviewed the creation and faith eras.

Now let's review the dispensation of law. This era included all the prophets, judges, kings, and details of how God began to use men to communicate His message to them. It was during this era that God caused the jackass to turn around and talk to Balaam. I don't know about you, but if I were riding a donkey, and it turned around and spoke to me. Believe me, it would get my attention. God did many unreal things during the dispensation of the law. One time, he caused the waters of a large river to roll back and allowed the children of Israel to cross over to the other side. The river not only rolled back, but the children of Israel walked across on dryland.

During this era, God enacted His power on many occasions. Usually, God selected one man to lead His nations. One man God chose to lead the Israelites into the dispensation of the law was Moses. Even during the dispensation of faith, God selected one man, Abraham, to lead and establish new nations on earth. Again, in my opinion, God was either trying to find a way to redeem man, or He was conditioning man to accept God's plan of redemption. If I read the Scriptures correctly, the dispensation of law was the first outlet in God's plan that allowed man to have a means of salvation if they followed the law.

Let me explain how I read this. All those who followed the law, after they died, were sent to a place called paradise where they would later be given an opportunity to become part of those redeemed from earth. It seems to me that God made the law where man had to be very sincere just to follow the law. The law seemed to be based a lot on *blood*. Blood of innocent animals was to be offered as a sacrifice before God would even listen to man's petitions. There was one occasion where God allowed Satan to take the life of all firstborn in the land. However, He made a provision where the children of Israel could escape this decree. He instructed the children of Israel to kill a lamb and smear the blood of this lamb over the door of their houses. Then when the death angel saw this blood, he would pass over that household, and the firstborn would be spared. I was just thinking about America as I read this in the Bible. We have become so relaxed in our belief in God that if we had to offer a blood sacrifice just to get God's attention, I doubt that God's mercy would prevail, much less His favor. I am sure that those covered by the law were able to dig deep into the *measure of faith* that God put into them to gain enough trust in God to follow the law. On the same measure, I know there are those in America who are finding a trust in God and a belief in their salvation through Jesus Christ. Remember the Scripture I quoted earlier: "Trust in the Lord with all your heart, lean not to your own understanding, and in all your ways, acknowledges Him, and He shall direct your path" (KJV).

Moses was selected by God to lead God's people out of a bondage that they were under in the land of Egypt. One thing about Moses, he seemed to be very hardheaded, even to the point that God had to cause a bush to catch on fire (strange thing about this bush, it never burned up) to get Moses's attention. When God finally got Moses's attention, God told him to go and call together all the leaders of Israel and tell them that the Lord, the God of their ancestors, the God of Abraham, Isaac, and Jacob, had appeared to him. An interesting point that the Scriptures point out was that Moses, even after experiencing the burning bush, still questioned his ability to lead. God had to further assure Moses that He (God) was the overall leader.

You know what God did? It was another one of those things, a lot like the talking ass. God told Moses to throw his staff down to the ground; and when he did, the staff turned into a snake. The Scripture relates that Moses was terrified and turned and ran away. I can't say that I would have reacted any differently if I tossed a stick down to the ground and it turned into a snake. I don't cater to snakes in the first place. God called Moses back and told him to take hold of the snake's tail. When Moses picked it up by the tail, it turned back into a staff. Now remember I told you that during this dispensation, God did many things that seemed unreal; this was one of those things.

In the next chapter, we will talk about how God no longer had to be limited to selecting one man to bring people into the kingdom of God. He has now made a means that God can dwell and communicate personally with each and every man. That happens to be the dispensation that we, in America, live under.

Keep in mind, we are still talking about the dispensation of law. After God finally convinced Moses to take the bull by the horn, he delivered His children out of bondage. This wasn't an easy chore, and I won't go into details about all the things God had to do to soften the hard-hearted Pharaoh who was the leader of the Egyptians.

Get this: God even had to turn the water into blood. Wouldn't that get the attention of America? There is already a concern that there will be enough water on earth. Can you imagine the panic if our water turned into blood? I shiver at the thought!

Through a series of events, God finally brought the children out from under the bondage of Pharaoh, and they were on their way to the promised land. You could even point to a resemblance to our forefathers (pilgrims) and their wandering on the ocean blue. One interesting thing happened as the children of Israel were being chased by Pharaoh after they left Egypt. With Pharaoh and his army closing in on them, they came to a large river. God told Moses to touch his staff to the water, and the water rolled back. Then Moses led the children of Israel through the river on dry ground. Seeing this, Pharaoh made a decision to follow the Israelites and led his army into the "dry" river. As soon as the Egyptian Army was fully into the river, guess what? God released the water, and the entire Egyptian Army was destroyed. What a great example of how God's power controls the universe. God led Pharaoh and his army into the Red Sea when they were hot on the trail of the Israelites. However, instead of the water being rolled back, when Pharaoh led his army into the sea, the water came down as a mighty rushing lion and destroyed Pharaoh and his army. You would think this is the end of the story, but keep in mind that God was trying to mold man into a path of salvation (the promised land). It just so happened man was still confined to

"I can handle this job all by myself"—just a thought. And isn't this true to form with what is taking place in America today? We have reached such a state of apathy that we no longer acknowledge God, and very few of us have enough faith in God to trust that God is still in control.

Let me tell you what happened to the Israelites. They wandered around in the wilderness for forty years and were only eleven miles (or days) from the promised land. Again, isn't this comparable to America? God allowed our forefathers to find a new land and build this nation on liberty, justice, and pursuit of happiness and now some four hundred years later, we are still wandering around, trying to find a simpler life. This group is against that group. Everyone is crying peace but never finding it. Neighbors are against neighbors, and our three-class system is slowly converting to a two-class system. The poor gets poorer, and the rich gets richer. Our promised land has been hit with floods, hurricanes, earthquakes, and fires; about the only thing left is the burning sulfur.

After forty years, the Israelites were led into the promised land. However, Moses was not allowed to lead the people into the land of milk and honey because he failed to follow the instruction God had given to him. God selected another man to lead the Israelites into the promised land. However, before Moses's death, God gave Moses a new dispensation in the form of what we now refer to as the Ten Commandments. These commandments were very simple and were given as a pattern for man to live by.

> The first of these commandments was to love God with all your heart and put no other gods before Him.
> The second commandment was not to take God's name in vain.
> The third commandment was to keep the Sabbath holy.
> The fourth was to honor your father and mother.
> The fifth was, not to murder or kill.
> The sixth was not to commit adultery.

Seventh was not to steal.

Eighth was not to testify falsely against your
    neighbor.

Ninth was not to covet your neighbor's wife.

Tenth was not to covet your neighbor's house or
    land.

God told Moses to teach these to all the people and to have parents teach them to their children.

Our forefathers took these commandments to heart. And in founding this great nation, they displayed them where everyone could see and adhere to them. In fact, they embedded them on courthouses, schools, on government buildings, etc. Here is the kicker. There is a force in America that is demanding that these commandments be taken off and out of all government functions.

Just recently, there was a judge who was ordered by the court to remove the commandments from his courthouse. And when he refused, he was ousted from his judgeship. *"How high's the water, Mama?"*

The Ten Commandments seemed to be the first step that God had made to guide man toward redemption. They also put into force a new dispensation. This is what I call the dispensation of the law. No doubt, God was very concerned that all men were created equal. And with the law, He had only put a temporary fix on salvation. In the next chapter, we will discuss how God's plan for salvation was finally solidified. I call it the dispensation of grace.

DISPENSATION OF GRACE

I can only offer my opinion on how the dispensation of grace came about. As I said before, we can only gather our own thoughts when the Scripture doesn't give details. We do know from the Scriptures that God is a triune being. This is evidenced throughout the Bible. After God created the heavens and the earth, the Scripture relates that God said, "Let us make man." This tells me that there were more than one involved. Then other Scriptures relate to God as God the Father, God the Son, and God the Holy Spirit. Since there are very little details about God and how they communicated, I am taking a privilege by being the author and expending some of my explorations of how God came up with the plan of salvation.

Of course, I am only offering my views; and again, I have no way of proving this, nor do I have Scripture to back it up. However, I would say to you that my opinion is probably as good as any other.

I can see God (the Father, the Son, and the Holy Spirit) discussing how, and what, they had to do to make a plan of redemption for man. No doubt, they talked about how they created man and made him a free-willed individual. Then they discussed how man chose to ignore God. And at this time, they could only find one man with grace, and they made a decision to destroy all creation, except this man and his family by way of a flood. After that, they gave man a measure of faith that pointed man toward God. This didn't seem to be the answer, so they installed a new plan of redemption that was designed by God to direct man a little more toward God. This plan gave man some means to exercise his free will by adhering to God's Commandments.

God (the Father, the Son, and the Holy Spirit) continued to discuss how they could provide a sacrifice to atone for man's sins against

God. I can see Jesus (the Son of God) speaking up and offering Himself as a sacrifice. If I can be afforded a little more imagination, I see Jesus pleading His case and confirming to God (the Father) that He really wanted to do this because He loved man as much as the Father did. Bottom line, they agreed that God the Son would go to earth as a man and be born of a virgin and would offer Himself to die on a cross so man could be redeemed from their sins. This would also provide God a direct means of communication between man and God. The overall plan was that after the Son died on the cross, He would return to heaven and would then send God the Holy Spirit to dwell in any man who accepted Jesus as the Son of God. This opened a direct means of communication between God and man. Since man was created in the image of God, he also was a triune being. God made man a physical man (body), a spiritual man (spirit), and gave him a soul when God breathed into man and made him a living soul.

During His time on earth, Jesus made it His mission to explain His reason for being on earth and left no doubt that He was the Son of God. One thing He said, and it was recorded in Scripture, that He was the way, the truth, and the life, and the only way man could come to God the Father was through Him.

> For God so loved the world that he gave his only
> son, so that everyone who believes in Him will
> not perish but have eternal life. (NLT)

No need to go into any more detail about the dispensation of grace. This tells it about as well as it could be explained.

To carry my imagination a little further into the conversation between God the Father, God the Son, and God the Holy Spirit, it could have continued like this. After God the Father agreed to send Jesus (God the Son) to offer this plan of salvation to man, He asked Jesus what He had in mind. Jesus replied that He would go down to earth and become a Son of Man and would only use the same powers that were available to man. No doubt, the Holy Spirit spoke up and said, "You mean you would not be able to use your heavenly power? Do you know how much you will have to endure?" No doubt God the Father asked Jesus if *He was sure He wanted to do this. Jesus, fully knowing what He was doing, again related that He loved man as much as God the Father did. I'm sure they all agreed that this could be the ultimate plan of redemption to man.*

But if I read it right, *redemption was not the only problem God had with man. There seemed to be a gap in communication between God and man. Remember the dispensation of creation when God could find only one man who trusted in God? All the others refused to accept and believe in God when God told them, through Noah, that He was going to bring rain in such abundance that the earth and all living things would be destroyed by a flood. They refused to believe such a ridiculous prediction. This was especially true since, up to this time, it had never rained, and all the moisture came from the ground by way of dew.*

Then under the dispensation of faith, man's communication from God was still limited to a one-on-one, usually with God selecting one man who had determined faith. It seems to me that God either had to talk to man personally or use men who were chosen by God to speak for Him. Oh, I forgot, God did use a donkey to talk to man. This was under a different dispensation, and nowadays, man wouldn't even listen if God tried to talk to them through their ass. (Have you ever had your ass talk to you?)

If I might continue my exploration of the conversation of the Godhead, no doubt, they all were exploring how to go about sending Jesus to become man. I'm sure God the Father once again outlined to Jesus how different it would be to limit Himself to man's power. I can see the Holy Spirit speaking up with an idea. He asked the Father if there could be a way that He could visit Jesus and enact His power through Jesus. It was possibly at this time they began to put together a plan that would allow God or the kingdom of God to dwell in the spirit of Man. Up until this time, there was no way man could speak directly to God. Man had a free will and was able to do what he pleased but had no way to ask God if he was doing the right thing. They agreed that Jesus would take upon Himself to become a man and would give Himself as an ultimate sacrifice. This would open the door for the Holy Spirit to personally baptize those who accepted Jesus Christ as their Savior, giving them heavenly powers.

At this point, the Godhead put their heads together and came up with a complete plan of redemption. I think the first thing the Godhead had to decide on was to determine how Christ would take on the form of a man. I'm sure they were aware of man's expectation of how a king would come and deliver mankind and how this king would rule on earth. Knowing this, God had to figure out a way that Jesus could be placed on earth without a lot of fanfare. They decided that Jesus had to be born as a man. To do this, they selected an innocent girl to be the mother of Christ. They selected a young woman, not yet married, and allowed the Holy Spirit to plant a seed that would cause this young girl to become pregnant, and God sent an angel to announce to her that the child she would bear would be the Savior of man. The angel went on to tell her that she should call this man-child, Jesus.

Finally, God chose to send Jesus to be born as a man, and they elected to send Him to earth in a very humble setting, not anything like man had expected Him to appear. He would become part of a normal family and would grow up in an earthly environment and for His first thirty years would not have any godly powers available. At the age of thirty, Jesus would begin His ministry. This ministry would be enacted through a baptism in water, and at that time, the Holy Spirit would ascend and baptize Christ with God's Holy Spirit and anoint Him with power from heaven. This would be a forerunner to God sending His Holy Spirit to dwell in man's spirit, thus giving man not only a plan of salvation but it would give man the guidance from the Holy Spirit and, for the first time, allow man to submit to God's will and direction.

When you think of how much God gave just to provide a means of redemption for man and then to evolve to the world today that works hard to convince men that God does not exist just seems unreal. Personally, I am so thankful to live under this dispensation of grace and to know that God is so good to allow me to live in a country that I can excite that free will that God endowed to me. *God bless America!*

The Bible so adequately outlines this dispensation of grace when Christ tells the disciples about eternal life. The disciples were troubled when Christ told them He would be betrayed by one of them and that the time had come for Him to return to glory. Here's how Christ explained to them the dispensation of grace. He first assured them that this was all in God's plan, and they should not be troubled. He went on to offer them comfort and told them they should trust Him because He had to go to prepare a place for them. To quote the Scripture directly: "Let not your hearts be troubled. You believe in God, believe also in me. In my Father's house are many mansions. If it were not so, I would have told you. I go to prepare a place for you" (KJV).

This dispensation of grace, because of Christ's sacrifice, provided man a plan of redemption and allowed man to once again find favor in the eyes of God.

Up to this time, God seemed to have a problem with man. This was evidenced when God repented that He had made man (Genesis 6:6). Again, we have very little knowledge about the dispensation of creation. We don't know how advanced they were. It was during this era that Scripture records the oldest man to live on the earth. He was 969 years old. When I think of how much technology man has invented in the last 100 years (airplane, TV, computers, cell phones, etc.), it makes me wonder how advanced man was prior to the great flood. We have no way of knowing; it just isn't recorded in the Bible. We do know that after the flood, God limited man's life on earth to 120 years. The Scripture in the sixth chapter of Genesis evidences this when God said, "My Spirit will not contend with man forever, for he is mortal, his days will be a hundred and twenty years."

God started all over after the flood. He made a decision not to destroy man again. This was when he found Abraham, whom God called a great man of faith. It was Abraham whom God chose to become the father of the nation of Israel. But God still had a problem with man and was still having a hard time communicating with man. In modem-day terms, we would classify man as being hardheaded, and the only thing that carried man through this era was faith. Even Abraham, with his faith, jumped ahead of God several times. But let's be fair, he did not have the Scriptures to direct him. Take the Scripture: "Trust in the Lord with all your heart, and lean not to your own understanding." There was a time when Abraham could have used this word. When Abraham was up in the years and his wife was past childbearing age, God told Abraham that he and his wife would have a son who would continue as leader of God's people. Abraham just couldn't compute this in his own understanding.

He decided to help God out and took his wife's maid to have his son. As a result of Abraham's leaning to his own understanding, God allowed the nation of Israel to be divided into two nations. When unreal things happen, even today, we have a hard time accepting that God's plan needs to be worked. Too many are working hard to plan God's work instead of working God's plan. Also, under the dispensation of faith, man had to follow God by walking in his own faith. Personally, I like the fact that we now live under the dispensation of grace and can, if we chose, walk under the direction of God's faith. This might be a good time to tell you of the fruits that man can bear by walking under the directions of the Holy Spirit. The Bible tells us that "when the Holy Spirit controls our lives, He will produce this kind of fruit in us: love, joy, peace, patience, kindness, goodness, faithfulness, gentleness, and self-control" (NLT).

Needless to say, man's faith just wasn't enough, and he had no way of drawing direction from God. There was a conflict with God's law. Under the dispensation of the law, God recognized that without some direction that man could follow, God had to give some guideline for man to follow. At that time, God personally wrote on a tablet and gave Ten Commandments to Moses for man to follow. Also, God established a semiform of salvation to those who followed the commandments. If I understand the Scriptures correctly, when Christ died on the cross, He told one of the men, who was also being crucified, that he would be with Him in paradise. That tells me that there was a holding place where all those who obeyed the law were sent and were given a chance to accept Christ as their Savior. According to the Scripture, after Christ was crucified, He went and preached to the spirits in prison. It isn't really clear who these spirits were that Christ preached to, but if you recall the words of Jesus, "I am the way, the truth and the life and no man comes to the Father except through me," this being the case, all those who lived under the dispensation of faith and the law had to be given an opportunity to accept Christ as their Savior. To be honest with you, I don't know what happened to those covered by the dispensation of creation. The Bible does say that only eight people were saved. There is no way of knowing if this applied to their salvation from the flood or if it included eternal life.

Since I have already injected many of my thoughts on how the dispensation of grace came about—and again, I caution you that this is my concept—let's carry it a little further. I would like to share with you what this grace means to me. To me, it is a lot more than just salvation, although this was God's way of offering man redemption for his sins. And if that was all Grace was, I would be forever grateful.

However, if I read and understand it right, grace gives me not only freedom from condemnation but provides me with life abundantly! Abundant life means that I have more than enough of everything I need. Add to this abundant life those fruits of the Spirit I listed above and the fact that if there is a hell, I won't have to spend my eternal life there. In addition, I can have a blessed hope that heaven is a real place. And not only do I escape going to hell, but I will go to heaven. Although this dispensation of grace didn't recreate man, there was a rebirth of man's spirit. According to the Bible, when we accept Christ as our Savior, we are born again. In fact, there is a story in the Bible where a man questioned Christ when Christ used the term born-again. This man asked Jesus how that could be. Here is how Jesus answered him: "The truth is no one can enter the kingdom of God without being born of water and the Spirit." Humans can reproduce only human life, but the Holy Spirit gives new life from heaven. So don't be surprised at my statement that you must be born again. Just as you can hear the wind but can't tell where it comes from or where it is going, so you can't explain how people are born of the Spirit (NLT). Needless to say, this man still didn't fully understand.

Let me offer my own thoughts on this, and I have come up with this interpretation from the study of several Scriptures. This is also my understanding of what the dispensation of grace brought to mankind. First of all, remember my accounting of how God decided to firmly offer a plan of redemption to man. He first created man, then

He established a measure of faith in man, and under the law, He gave man a list of rules to abide by (the Ten Commandments). Up to this point, it was clear that God had to bring a means of final redemption so man could prove his love to God.

There are a couple of things, according to the Bible, that God puts a lot of emphasis on. Remember how we expressed that when our forefathers founded this nation, they built it of faith, hope, and love. From my study, I believe God had several things that he had to put into place after he gave man a free will. Without these being available to man, there could never be a confirmed allegiance to God and God's love. Let me put it this way, love can never be one-sided. In order for love to be consummated, both parties have to participate. If you don't believe this, try making love to a chair. You can pick up the chair and wrap your arms around it and kiss it and love on it, but since it cannot love you back, neither you nor the chair will get a thing out of it. It was quite clear that during the dispensations of creation, faith, and the law, man just wasn't responding to God's love. Remember the reason God made man in the first place? He gave man free will so man could elect to love God without being forced. I believe God decided that He would give man a clear plan of redemption (or some might call it an incentive) to love Him.

God had given to man the measure of faith. He had given a set of rules for man to follow. And from what I read from the Bible, God had made a covenant with man never to force God's *will* on man. Since we were made in the image of God, we (according to the Scriptures) were created with a spiritual body, living in a physical body, and God breathed into man and made man a living soul. As I studied the Bible, I learned that life could only take place through the flow of blood. Since we seem to understand more about the physical blood that flows through our fleshly bodies, we have learned that when this blood stops flowing, life ends. Then as I studied more about God, I learned how blood seems to be involved with everything that concerned God.

The first recording of how much importance God placed on blood started with the story of Cain and Abel. If you have read the accounting of Cain and Abel, God recognized Abel's offering of a blood sacrifice and was not pleased with Cain's gift of farm products. This is another one of those things that the Scriptures give us very little detail, but it is very clear that God required a blood offering. Throughout the Bible, blood was emphasized as a means of offering a sacrifice to God. The dispensation of grace proved to be the ultimate sacrifice to bring man to God through a blood sacrifice from His Son. Three things God seems to require are faith, which is belief; blood, which is life; and trust, which is love.

Now let me give you my interpretation of what Jesus was telling the man about being born again. God had to find a way to draw man close to Him. In the Bible, He tells us if we will draw close to Him, He will draw close to us. When God sent his Son to die on the cross, Christ not only shed His blood, but He proved that, as a man, we could have the confidence that God's blood could flow in our spirit, a lot like that measure of faith God had put into man. In simple terms, if we accept and believe in Christ, at that moment, our spirit is born into the kingdom of God. I'm not going to tell you I completely understand this because the only way I can compare things of the spiritual is through physical life experiences. However, remember the measure of faith God gave us; well this gives me a means to accept God (through faith) and believe in Him.

We are born of water when we are birthed on earth by a physical mother. This is why it was so important for Jesus to be born through a woman. Since we are a spiritual body as well as a physical body, God has now made a provision that we can now be born as a spiritual being. When we accept Christ as our Savior, and God's lifeblood flows through our spirit, then according to God's Word, we are born again. (Read chapter 3 of John's gospel.)

Let me carry this a little further by letting you know that, in addition to the blood flow, God has taken our unique makeup and sent His Holy Spirit to dwell in our inner spirit, and we can now have godly powers available to us. Again, I don't fully understand this, but I am able to accept it through faith. One scripture that confirms this was made by Jesus when He walked on earth. He said, "These things and even greater things shall you do after I am returned to the heavenly Father." *Wow*! I have to assume that that includes walking on water if needed.

I am sure that God recognized that man would continue to rebel against Him, and He had to make a provision that man could be forgiven of his sins. At the same time, God made a way man could enter into the very presence of God by a rebirth of man's spirit. I call this the dispensation of grace.

Grace is so simple to obtain and is explained by the scripture: John 3:16. Many things in the Bible are hard to understand, but this scripture is very simple. You believe, and grace is given. Sometimes we struggle to understand God and give reason to why things happen. Many times, the scripture is written to give us a little insight but gives us very few details. Maybe God figured He would tell us what He thought we should know. An example is, where is heaven? If you ask anyone, even the learned scholars, where heaven is located, they may speculate, but they really don't know. How simple is this: "For God so loved the world that He gave His only Son, and whosoever believes in Him shall have everlasting life" (KJV)?

Since I am already out on the limb, let me offer my thoughts on the dispensation of grace.

When and how does a man become saved? Can a man accept Christ at the very moment he dies? If there is deathbed salvation, why does the Bible place so much on serving God and making God the Lord of our lives? Is John 3:16 inclusive? Think about it! It says that whosoever believes will not perish but have everlasting life. Does that mean all we must do to go to heaven is believe that Jesus Christ is the Son of God? Why does the Scripture go on to say that if we repent of our sins, we will be saved? Is there a difference between being saved and making Him Lord of your life? This is something really simple that you might have to study hard to get an answer. What does it mean to *serve* God? Should we be standing on a corner with a sign in our hand saying "repent, or you will go to hell"? How holy must we become to serve God? Again, I must offer my opinion, and I have thought a great deal about it, but it seems to me that Jesus gave us the answer to serving Him when He gave us a new commandment to love one another as He has loved us. I have to believe that this is how we *serve* God.

Even if you say you believe in the Bible and that it is the inspired Word of God, it still becomes hard at times to find answers to the questions above. There just doesn't seem to be any black-and-white answer. How do we find a religion that has all the answers? We have been talking about the dispensation of grace in this chapter, but we must initiate a lot of faith to accept and believe that salvation can be so easy. It is truly *amazing grace, how sweet the sound; we have no less days to sing God's praise than when we first began.* Everlasting life can be yours. *Whosoever believes shall have everlasting life!*

It's Time to Rumble—
Put on the Gloves!

Rumble—now that is an interesting word. *Webster* defines it this way: "to make a dull continued sound or a low heavy continued sound." Another definition might be that "to rumble" is an invitation to get America back on track. If you refer back to the preface of this book, it started off by quoting Psalm 100.

> Shout with joy to the Lord, O earth! Worship the Lord with gladness. Come before Him, singing with joy. Acknowledge that the Lord is God. He made us, and we are His. We are His people, the sheep of His pasture.

It seems to go on to give an up-to-date message to America's church. "Enter His gates with thanksgiving; go into His courts with praise. Give thanks to Him and bless His name. For the Lord is good. His unfailing love continues forever, and His faithfulness continues to each generation." It is time for the church to recognize and understand that God's faithfulness extends to our generation and beyond.

We have determined that faith, hope, and love are currently not being extended to our generation, and the church is not operating under the gifts of the Spirit. *Webster* says gifts are given. If that is the case, since the church no longer has the gifts in operation, how do we get the gifts back into the church? Some have said that we should seek the gifts. I can't find anywhere the Scriptures instruct us to seek the gifts. There are a couple of places it tells us we can ask for the gifts; but as *Webster* relates, gifts are given.

As we determined in the previous chapter, it is imperative that we restore the gifts back to the church because as I read it, without gifts, the church has no power. In addition, if the church is going to win the war between the church and state, it must have the strength that comes with the gifts. What do we do to bring the church back to a place of clout with community?

A good place to start is to enact Psalm 100 back into our lives. How long has it been since you just shouted with joy to the Lord? Do you worship the Lord with gladness? How often do you come before God and sing with joy? How many Americans acknowledge that the Lord is God and recognize that He made us, and we are His creation? Do you regularly "enter His gates," or in everyday language, do you go to church? How often do you pray or give God thanksgiving? If we don't seek the gifts, how do we get them? In simple terms, there is a Scripture that gives more direction than any clergy or minister could ever give you. It is found in Matthew 6:33. In the New King James version, it says, "For your heavenly Father knows that you need all these things. But seek first the kingdom of God and His righteousness, and all these things shall be added to you." I like the way the Living translation puts it: "Your heavenly Father already knows all your needs, and He will give you all you need day to day if you live for Him and make the Kingdom of God your primary concern." Remember how we discussed that the kingdom of God is within you?

The key is, how do we live for Him? If there is one thing the church needs to do, it is to acknowledge that there is a difference between making Christ your Savior and making Him Lord of your life. If you could survey the churches and ask them to instruct you on how to serve God, I have no doubt that you would have a thousand different answers. Some would tell you that you must spend three hours a day on your knees praying. Another might tell you that you have to read the Bible through ten times. Another would say you have to go to church. Still another might say that you have to keep the Ten Commandments. Some might say you have to speak in tongues, and still another might say don't smoke, drink, or run around. I would challenge you to find someone who will answer the question like Christ did. Just before His death on the cross, He told the disciples that He was giving them a new commandment: "Love each other, just as I have loved you. You should love each other." He went on to say that love for one another will prove that you are one of His disciples. Isn't that what we become when we make Christ the Lord of our lives? The answer is love. We talked about it in the previous chapter and agreed that there is very little love for our fellowman in America. Think with me a moment. Wasn't this what caused the great Civil War? It was brother against brother, sister against sister, children against parent, neighbor against neighbor, etc. As I related earlier, we are not far from that state of being in America today. If you don't believe it, just look at what is currently going on in Washington. True, it hasn't reached bloodshed (maybe a fistfight), but don't kid yourself; there is a civil war going on, and the base root is between church and state. Even those who profess to believe in God are at war with each other.

Let me tell you a personal story that almost caused me to quit attending church. As a youngster my parents attended a church that had a set of rules that not even those in heaven could live by. I will never forget when one of the saints cornered me and told me how I needed to be careful playing football and doing all those worldly things. Now to give you a picture (at least this is what I say), this lady wore a Pentecostal bun and never cut her hair. I guess this was because there is a Scripture that says it is shameful for a woman to cut her hair. That's not all; she didn't even shave her legs! In the eyes of others in the church, she was a holy woman. However; after she cornered me, I began to watch her. Can you believe that this woman disliked another woman in the same church so much that she wouldn't even sit by her? It didn't take me long to learn that if I followed man and his holiness, I might have a hard time just living on earth. I'm sure that I am not alone in not connecting with the radical belief of some of these Christians. This couldn't be what Christ was talking about when He said we could have life and life more abundantly. Did you know there was a group, and I understand they are still in existence, which took the Scripture where Christ was explaining the Great Commission? He was giving an example of the power that could be available to His disciples, and He told them they would be able to handle snakes with safety, and it wouldn't hurt them. You guessed it; one man read this and started a religion. If that's what I have to do to live more abundantly, you can forget it!

It has always been a mystery to me why Christians still live under the law. In my study of the New Testament, I learned that the majority of it was written by the apostle Paul. During his lifetime, the spiritual law was also the physical law of the land. If you will study it carefully, you will find that many things Paul wrote were based on living under the law. What is hard for me to understand is that Jesus said He didn't come to do away with the law but that He came to fulfill the law. As Christians, we think that we still must live by the law. A good example of this is the biblical teachings on divorce and remarriage. Examples can be found in Christ's teachings in Matthew 6:32: "But I say that a man who divorces his wife, unless she has been unfaithful, causes her to commit adultery, and anyone who marries a divorced woman commits adultery." This was what the law of the land taught, but it also allowed those caught in adultery to be stoned to death. Some in the church have placed so much emphasis on this that if a minister in their religion divorces his wife and remarries, he is excommunicated. Where does forgiveness come into play?

Under the dispensation of grace, the Bible teaches that we are forgiven of our sins, or mistakes, and they are never remembered against us again. If we die, even though we are sinners, we are sinners saved by grace, and we will still go to heaven. It also says no sin can enter the kingdom of heaven. My question is this: Why can't we be forgiven here on earth, or do we have to wait until we get to heaven to be forgiven? In my opinion (here I go again), man has no concept of forgiveness and an abundant life. Just a thought! Did I misread the scripture that says my sins—past, present, and all my future sins— are forgiven? If God can forgive, why can't man?

Back to where we were. Why do we need the gifts of the Spirit directing us? Again, to quote Jesus, He told the disciples that after they had received the Comforter that the Comforter would teach and guide them into all truth. For those of you who may not know who the Comforter is, He is the Holy Spirit. The Holy Spirit brings the gifts of the Spirit to the church and the fruits of the Spirit to those who follow Christ. Again, I give you more of my opinion and how I believe the Holy Spirit comes into our life when we make a decision to make Christ the Lord of our life. At that time, we enter the kingdom, and faith, hope, and love become abundant with us.

When the gifts are in full operation in the church, then the fruits of the Spirit are seen in the individual members. This might be a good time to once again review the gifts and their functions. I know I have already gone over these gifts, but unless these gifts are restored to the church, there cannot be a revival.

The gifts can be broken down into groups of three. First group would be the intellectual gifts. They are the gift of knowledge, wisdom, and faith. The second group would be the power gifts. They include the gift of miracles, discernment, and divine healing. The last group could be called the speaking gifts. These are the gift of prophecy, tongues, and interpretation.

Let's take time to explore each of these individually. First the gift of knowledge: Although this is a silent gift, it is one of the most important in understanding the Word and knowing the difference between right and wrong. Although this gift and all the others are executed by and given through the individual, it is essential in the operation of the church. Lack of knowledge may be why many of the churches are operating without any direction. Come to think of it, this could be why the children of Israel wandered around in the wilderness for forty years and were only eleven miles from the promised land. The next gift, the gift of wisdom, according to Proverbs, is what God founded the earth on. In reviewing this gift, I find the Scripture refers to wisdom as being better than silver, rubies, riches, and honor. Wisdom was what King Solomon asked for when God appeared to Solomon in a dream and told him he could ask for anything and God would give it to him. Instead of asking for a long life, riches, or honor, he asked for wisdom. God was so pleased by this that He not only gave him wisdom but also gave him riches and honor. Without wisdom, the church can easily fall into serving two masters.

> For you will hate one and love the other, or be devoted to one and despise the other. You cannot serve both God and money. (NL1)

The next gift is the gift of faith. Without faith, we cannot please God. Then there are the gifts of healing, discerning of spirits (my interpretation of this gift is to know if it is of God or some other spirit), and working of miracles. This gift, the working of miracles, is often expressed through a miraculous happening that usually is initiated for the protection of the body of believers. Let me give you an example from the Old Testament when God caused the waters to be rolled back to save the children of Israel, as recorded in Exodus 14. Finally, there are gifts of prophecy, speaking in tongues, and the interpretation of tongues. The apostle Paul defined prophecy as a way of edifying, exhorting, and comforting the church. We have previously talked about tongues and interpretation of tongues.

If I had to pick out a couple of scriptures that could go a long way in restoring the gifts to the church, I would have to choose Proverbs 3:5–6.

> Trust in the Lord with all your heart and lean not to your own understanding: In all your ways acknowledge Him, and He shall direct your path.

The other Scripture is found in 2 Chronicles 7:14.

> If my people who are called by my name will humble themselves and pray and seek my face and turn from their wicked ways, then I will hear from heaven, and will forgive their sin and heal their land. (NKJV)

These Scriptures were written at different times and directed toward different nations. Let's look at how they fit our nation today. Just as the scripture in Proverbs says the first step is to rekindle a trust in God, you cannot doubt for a second that America needs to be humbled. It seems God has to allow America to undergo humbling times ever so often. Sometimes this experience comes in the form of war, depression, recession, earthquakes, hurricanes, fires, and other disasters to bring America down off a high. It usually brings a unity, which results in Americans praying and seeking God's face. This prayer in turn causes man to turn from his wicked ways. It might be time for us to humble ourselves, pray, "seek first the kingdom of God," and ask God to forgive our sins and heal our land.

A quick review of this is (1) humble ourselves, (2) pray, (3) seek God, (4) turn from our wicked ways, and (5) ask for forgiveness. This is a straightforward spiritual message to the church. We have taken Spiritual guidance directly from God's word. Now let's review what we can do to bring revival back to the church.

We must find a way to educate our children and reinstate God and godly things back into our nation. It doesn't take a rocket scientist to know that our educational system is failing. And instead of being taught about God, our public-school system is being coached toward atheism. At the same time, unlike when our forefathers established this land, the church no longer is a part of educating our children. Church is deeply involved in civil wars that have reached into the schools. And instead of parents being in control of educating our children, we have turned it over to the government. Take a moment and let's explore a new idea of a parent-church schooling. Not only can this be an innovative way to educate our children, but it also could be a new revival to the church. Remember the verse, *without a vision, the people perish.*

An Evocative Approach to Education Parent-Church Schooling

Parent-church schooling (PCS) is not a new approach for our society. It actually came into being when the early pioneers established a formal means of teaching their children. Parents got together and recognized that they had to set up a program where their children could be taught reading, writing, and arithmetic under a formal format. They bound together and solicited the church for involvement. The final outcome was that the church building would be utilized during the week to house or provide classrooms, and in most cases, the parents elected the pastor or his wife as a teacher. This program not only proved to be an effective way to teach their children, but it allowed parents to become more involved in church activities and belief. Parents became a part of the church family, and they were able to achieve the last commandment that Christ gave to us: "Love one another as I have loved you, so you must love one another. All men will know you are my disciples if you love one another" (NIV).

PCS also would give the church a new way to promulgate the gospel of God to the children. It must be an offense to God that we have huge church facilities that have their doors closed except for one service on Sunday. Just think if we returned to the ways of early America and could utilize these church facilities during the week to house the (parent-operated and controlled) schools. That might be a start to solving some of our educational problems. In addition, it could be a step toward allowing parents to pull their children out of public school and reevaluate educating America's children. Not only would it give our children a new direction and allow them to follow a principle that was established by our forefathers, but also, it could become a new mission for the church. In addition, this could once again give the church a new commission since welfare is now under the control of the government instead of the church. The original mission of the church was to take care of the needy, poor, widows, and orphans. Keep in mind that PCS is not designed to eliminate public schools but to supplement them.

Under the PCS program, parents could choose a church of their own faith and could once again become active in a church. At the same time, they could educate their children to trust in God and know their children are being exposed to a renewed belief that there is a God. Also, the basic foundation of reading, writing, and arithmetic could be reinstated, and our children could be allowed time to grow up as God intended.

There has to be an answer to guide our children away from misguided thoughts that are resulting in their killing their classmates, their teachers, and themselves. Almost daily, there are reports of students beating up on each other or attacking teachers. America's parents must find a way to bring their children back into the fold and take more control in teaching and training their children. First step is to renew family life to our society. This will be a big struggle for most American families who are geared to both parents working just to make a living.

Has America reached a point of no return? Can family life ever be restored? Could Americans exist under a simpler life, such as one family car, one TV, one computer, and a one-car garage?

Are we spoiled to a point that our world would crumble if we are not able to keep up with our neighbors? A national poll recently revealed that a majority of Americans would welcome reverting to a much simpler life. However, only a few think they could financially afford to make their family a one-parent working family. Younger parents, when questioned how they felt about homeschooling their children, offered a large number of reasons why they could not find the time or meet the qualifications. Biggest excuse was that there was no way, with both parents working, that they could find time to homeschool their children. An overwhelming majority found a common ground that if they could find a way, they would remove their children from public schools and wouldn't hesitate to do it. All recognized that God has been taken out of the public schools. Based on this survey, it is evident that one of the largest obstacles that would be encountered in establishing a PCS program would be the working mom.

Unless Americans can install an educational system that will bring their children back to basics, the future of this great country may be facing destruction even greater than Katrina. (Katrina was the hurricane that caused the destruction of New Orleans.) Can America survive more disasters like the twin towers (9/11), earthquakes, and other catastrophes that have recently taken its toll on America? There seems to be a nonchalant attitude that has been instilled into our society that has caused Americans to care less about what they believe or believe in. When the pilgrims arrived at Plymouth Rock on that cold winter day, they brought with them a desire to find a new life. After a long trip, even though they were very tired, they had to take time to thank God when they viewed those spacious skies, with purple mountains and a majesty that reached across the fruited plains. They were well aware from whence they came and that God had led them to the promised land. There is a parallel story in the Bible that relates how the children of Israel were brought out of bondage, and God led them to a promise land. I am sure that our forefathers knew this story by heart and had determined that they would create a nation under a trust in God. In the constitution, they adopted and formulated a document that established a nation that would always display a belief in God. First thing, and it can be backed up by historical accounts, on their agenda was to construct a church. This church would not only serve as a place they could go to offer allegiance to their God, but this facility would double as a community meeting place.

These early pilgrims were well aware that they had to unite their efforts in order to survive the hardships they were to face in building a new nation. They put a lot of emphasis on their prior teachings to love one another, and they were conditioned to fellowship together.

Because of this, they formulated a schooling program that was set up a lot like they set in their constitution: *by the people, for the people, and of the people.* The community's church was used as a schoolhouse, and everyone joined together to make sure that children would be taught and trained to prepare them as future leaders. Every child had instilled in them the theme that they later put on the currency: "in God we trust." (It is interesting to note that some in America are working to get this taken off our money.) PCS could provide a new mission for the church.

Our churches don't have a growing problem; they have a glowing problem. Since the government took over the welfare program, only a few churches have attracted enough new people to reflect a growth pattern. Most churches are operating on a shoestring budget, and their parish is mostly made up of older and longtime members. Not many people in America can find a reason to join up with a church. There are still a few that feel they must attend a church to expose their children to God. Most have a hard time determining how a church can benefit them, and they find no reason to give a portion of their earnings to support a church facility. Government has so been geared to provide help to anyone who needs it, and the church is called on very little to meet a person's (even members') needs. It is sad to say that most churches no longer carry the favor of God.

It is time for the church to awake and put off its slumber, revise its vision, and combine that vision with God's universal vision to promulgate the gospel. Churches have failed to rotate their vision around the basic teaching that is stressed in the Bible: "Where there is no vision, the people perish" (KJV). It is a known fact that very few churches have any vision at all. Nowadays, most spend all their efforts in survival, and outreach to the community is a thing of the past. No longer do churches offer an exposure to God, and there is a tendency to ignore the importance of their responsibility to teach the Word of God to the children.

In the past fifty years, America has managed to go from a nation founded on God to a nation that has moved toward being an atheist country. We have installed too many laws that do not express the majority's point of view. Our school system is a prime example of this. There seems to be a state of apathy that has gripped America where family life requires both parents to work just to pay the bills. It is new cars, big houses, and a lifestyle that is over the head for most middleclass people. It has reached the point that the class system our forefathers set up has reverted from a three-class system of poor, middle-class, and rich to only a two-class system of poor and rich. Most families get so overloaded with life pressures to "keep up with the Joneses" that they can't find time for their children. As a result, our children are not being encouraged toward God and are not being "trained up in the way they should go." With the working mom, too many children are often left alone and find themselves so confused that, by the time they become teenagers, wind up committing suicide. Somehow, we must find a way to bring America back to the last commandment Christ gave us, that is to love one another, and let it start by training our children to love and respect others. Dust has accumulated on family Bibles, and very few, although they say they believe in God, could give you a reason why they believe in God. Instead of taking God out of our schools, we need to find a way to put Him back into our lives. Church, it's time to rumble!

It is a sad state of being when our children are not taught how to be Americans and can't even recite the Pledge of Allegiance. Very few teenagers know anything about how the constitution works, and most don't even know how to vote. Ask any of the younger people what party they belong to, and they usually will tell you they belong to the Republican or Democratic parties but couldn't give you any reason why they claim that party. It is the same way with belief in God; they say they believe in God, but not many can tell you why. The vast majority only know that they have been taught that there is a God and are satisfied to accept that what their ancestors told them was true. Parents today fail to recognize the importance of training and teaching a child and have skirted their responsibility by allowing their children to be taught and trained by a nursery day care worker. An old-time saying that lifetime beliefs and characteristics are usually formulated during the first six years of a child's life still holds true today. Wake up, parents. And for the sake of your children, take time out to ensure that your children are endowed with proper training through a coveted love that can only come from mom and dad. *God, bless our children.*

A lot of parents would be homeschooling their children, except for a lack of time, a feeling of being underqualified, along with recognizing the need for social involvement for their children. This coupled with being unable to control, supervise, discipline, and to make new adjustments to life. They have chosen to keep their children in public schools. Most parents are aware of the push to remove God from the school system, and many speak out against it; but very few have any alternative or power to do anything about it. It is quickly approaching the 100 percent mark where every parent is employed in fulltime jobs, and the only way they can find to pay the bills is for both husband and wife to work. Americans are making their children, and their children are being thrown out to the wolves. Families are no longer the focal point of our nation's endeavor, and it is sad to say that too many parents fail to stress the welfare of their children. Children are forced to grow up too fast. And by the time they reach their teens, they are stressed out. The result has produced disastrous effects on our children. Fast growth, fast food, and unsupervised living have created overstressed, overweight, unloved, and an apathetic attitude about life in our children.

With the fast moving and highly technical world, basic schooling of reading, writing, and arithmetic has almost become a thing of the past. By the time children start school, they are already operating a computer. If they are not on the computer, they spend the majority of their day glued to the television set. Without realizing it, parents are not putting any time or effort into training their children, and television and computers formulate the child's life. With a click of a button, children are being exposed to porn that would make their parents blush. Sex and violence are fed to them at an enormous pace. By the time children reach school age, they are already formulated in life and usually have no basic teaching toward God or trust in God.

They are sent off to school (or thrust into a raging world), and their little minds are just not able to put it together. By the time they reach their teens, many are ready to take their own lives, someone else's life, or find themselves seeking any means of escape from the pressure being put on them. Many find a way to elude some of this pressure by turning to drugs, alcohol, perverted sex, etc. Then when they get caught up in this trap, their parents just can't understand why or what caused them to do something like this.

Again, parents, wake up and get involved in training and teaching your children. We have to give our babies a chance to grow up. If you try to feed a steak to a baby, it will choke to death. Just as a baby needs time to grow up, get teeth, and learn to chew, a child's mind must have time to develop before it is crammed with a lot of technical things, like being involved with a computer. Did you know, many elementary schools no longer have recess time? For those of you who don't know what recess is, it is a time set aside where children can take a break and relax from the stress of the classroom. When a child is young, their brains must have a time-out to develop. Why do you think God made children to have short attention spans? God never intended that His children become adults by the time they are teenagers. It is sad to say that too many of our schools push too hard too fast. A lot of schools have taken the arts out and replaced it with computers. I have never understood why a child spends six to seven hours in a given day at school and then comes home with four hours of homework. Really, does that make sense to you? We have completely distorted the cliché that "all work and no play make Jack a dull boy" and turned it around to all work with no play will make Jack grow up faster. That is exactly what is happening in our public-school system. What is really sad is we are still graduating some students from high school who don't even know how to read and write.

In America, there is very little on-the-job training. Remember the distributive education (DE) schools had—and some still do— that allowed the students to work in the community to learn a trade. Like I said, some schools still have these programs; however, most students use this time to work as clerks or in fast foods just to make a few extra bucks. We have created a world where everybody wants to start in the workforce at an executive level instead of a gofer. In case you don't know what a gofer is, it is someone who follows direction of those in charge to get this or do this or "gofer" something the boss wants. *How high's the water, Mama?*—seven feet high and rising. Question is, what do we do about it? Parents can't homeschool with both husband and wife working. And how about the single parent? If you think the days of the working mom will ever go away, you might be living in a fantasy world. Let's face it; the working mom is here to stay. However, we must find a way to bring parents back to a hands-on training of their children. Parent-church schooling might be a means of breaking the ice and could also give the church a new mission or reason for existing. This is a program designed to bring parents back to personally teaching their children. The overall idea is to recreate a way to help the working mom spend more time teaching and training her children and provide a faith based parental love. In summary, it injects a parent's love into schooling and educating the child.

Parents

Under the parent-church schooling program, the first step to enact has to be made by the parents. PCS will only work if the parents are willing to give and adapt to a change in their lives. They must become knowledgeable and conscious that there is a force that is working overtime to destroy their children. Parents should be willing to make changes in their lifestyle to accommodate their children. Recognize that more time has to be given toward family life and, even though they are both working and trying to hold everything together, find a way to reinstate love toward their children. It is essential parents readjust their lives to include the welfare of their children, especially in the godly training and teaching of the child. We must put more emphasis on what our forefathers were so careful to address, and that is as recorded in the Bible: "Train up a child in the way he should go, and when he is old, he will not depart from it" (KJV). The next step is to get involved and become aware of what their children are being taught. Also, PCS will encourage parents who are not satisfied with how their children are schooled to personally get involved in the teachings and make sure the teacher fits their values. Parents should take time to study and review PCS and evaluate if it can be incorporated into their lifestyle. Instead of making excuses why they can't participate, find a way, for their children's sake, to spend one day a week with their children.

PCS is designed to allow the working mom or dad to personally get involved and give a hands-on touch (in educating their children). For example, did you know that the public schools have developed a test to give to high school students, and if they score high enough, the students will be put in a *government*-run program, and these students are trained and personally directed toward government? It has a likeness to the same type of schooling program used *by* communism to teach and train their children. Keep aware that there is a minority (less than 15 percent) that is working to remove God and any reference to Him from our society. One last note to parents: If there are agents and agencies trying to convert America to an atheist nation, the best way to accomplish it is to start *by* converting our children. But it is and will always be your responsibility to teach and train up your child. Selah!

Church

Awake, awake, church. Put off your slumber. Revise your vision, and the truth shall set you free. Combine your vision with God's universal vision to promulgate a belief in God.

Churches have failed to rotate their vision around the basic teaching according to Proverbs 29:18 (KJV): "Where there is no vision the people perish." As a result, many churches are failing. Parent-church schooling is a program that is designed to reinstate the knowledge of God's saving grace back into our children. In the book of Hosea 4:6, we are warned that God's people are destroyed for lack of knowledge (KJV). If our children are never told of God's love and are never exposed to the existence of God, then we should prepare ourselves for destruction.

Under the PCS program, churches could build in a faith class and teach about Christian heritage and expose the children to God and the Bible. Church history records how the first church was started when the apostle Peter preached his sermon on the day of Pentecost, and some three thousand believed and accepted Christ. According to the Bible, they joined with other believers in regular attendance at the apostles teaching sessions and at communion services and prayer meetings. It goes on to say that the whole city was favorable to them, and each day, God added to them all who were being saved.

In America today, the church, especially those who are still trying to witness the message of salvation through Jesus Christ, have found a lack of favor and are no longer experiencing a growth pattern. As with almost any organization, there is no place that the church can stand still. It is either growing or falling off. According to a recent survey, in the past twenty years, America's churches are experiencing a decline of up to 70 percent in attendance. As a result, our children are not exposed to things of God and have no training or knowledge of God. PCS could be a unique way for churches to increase attendance since only children of active members of that church can enroll.

One of the main purposes of PCS is to encourage parents to reunite with the church of their faith by enrolling their children into the PCS program. This way, they will be able to expose their children to God. As previously discussed, there are many parents who have been exposed to God and the church but are not passing this experience on to their children. Just look at the impact that the motion picture *The Passion of the Christ* had on the secular world. Family members, who had not been to church in years, were able to renew their belief in God by seeing the movie. It seemed to serve as a wake-up call to parents as to what is happening to their children and how there is a need to emphasize the message of God's salvation and encourage them to get into church.

But the question is, how do we get off the roller coaster? Parents are working; there is no extra time for children, church, and recreation. It is sad that families are trapped into a world that has learned to survive without the church. Most have heard of the push to extract God from the schools and that there is a small minority group that is trying to divide church and state. Thousands of parents would be homeschooling their children but can't find a way to give the time and effort required.

The PCS program with the church providing its facilities and utilizing voluntary members, along with parents taking one day a week to supervise, could offer a classroom atmosphere with godly training. Parents would be able to give a hands-on input and know that their children were not being exposed to teachings against the beliefs of the parents.

Through PCS, families could be encouraged to participate in church activities and fellowship. Once again, as it was in the earlier days, the church could become the central point in family activities.

By encouraging the parent-church schooling program, a church could redefine its vision and bring increased favor. They could use the PCS to add new members and rekindle the favor of God.

Without the church, America grows farther and farther away from the favor of God that was promised to those early pilgrims who endured a long voyage across the ocean to a promised land. What has happened to our nation is so well defined in a prophecy that was given through the prophet Hosea. It is so adequately stated in the Living Bible translation and fits America to a tee.

> The Lord has filed a lawsuit against you listing the following charges: there is no faithfulness, no kindness and no *knowledge of God* in your land. You swear and lie and kill and steal and commit adultery, there is violence everywhere, with one murder after another. That is why your land is not producing, it is filled with sadness and all living things grow sick and die and the animals, the birds and even the fish have begun to disappear. You are trying to pass the blame on to others and you should not point your finger at someone else. Don't point your finger at someone else and try to pass the blame! Look, you priests, my complaint is with you! As a sentence for your crimes, you will stumble in broad daylight, just as you might at night, and so will your false prophets. My people are being destroyed because they don't

> know me. It is your entire fault, you priests, for
> you yourselves refuse to know me. Now I refuse
> to recognize you as my priest. Since you have
> forgotten the laws of your God, I will forget to
> bless your children. The more priest there are, the
> more they sin against me. They have exchanged
> the glory of God for the disgrace of idols. (NLT)

In that same chapter, Hosea goes on to say that alcohol and prostitution have robbed the people of their brains.

I thought this was interesting in that it so describes what is happening to our church and our country today. At one place in this Scripture, he went on to say that not only the priests are wicked, but the people are wicked, and he will punish both for their ungodly deeds, for they have deserted the Lord and worshipped other gods.

If this doesn't motivate you to reinstate a schooling program for our children to include God and the church and find a way that parents can once again personally train up their children, well I'm just lost for words. Did you know that there are now over 330,000,000 people in America, and the majority of these are under thirty years of age? What is even more sad is that very few of those under thirty have attended church.

Church, parents need your help, but more importantly than that is you need their help. United we stand, divided we fall.

Schooling

Why is it that God gives special abilities to different people to do certain things? Why can one child play the piano and another can ride a horse? The Bible answers it this way: "It is God's way of equipping us to do a better work for God, thus building up the church and the body of Christ to a position of strength and maturity until finally we all believe alike about our salvation and become full grown in the Lord" (NLT). There is one place in the Bible where a young man by the name of Timothy is instructed to use the abilities God had given him and to put these abilities to work and to improve and grow in them. Did you know that the Bible also tells us that, in the last days, there will be teachers who will tell and teach lies? And since God does not inspire these teachers, and they listen to Satan more than God, their consciences would not even bother them.

If we have made such a big issue of taking God out of our schools, and we have hired teachers that have no belief in God, how can we train our children to be encouraged to use their God-given abilities?

If there is a war going on between church and state, and the state runs and controls our schools, those parents who still believe in God should be shaking in their boots.

To adequately train up a child in our Christian society, God has to be involved. Our problem is not our schools; it is more of a parenting problem. If our children are never introduced to God by their parents, how do we expect them to find God? In our present society, we have completely turned the training and teaching of our children over to schools, controlled by a government that forbids the mere mention of God. Schools are infiltrated with leaders and teachers who have been hired based on their academic skills and were never questioned about their moral backgrounds. No longer do our schools consider what a teacher believes or any past moral issues in the teachers' background. If they hold a teaching certificate, hire them!

Take a moment to review some recent headlines from America's newspapers:

Ex-swim club coach arrested on suspicion of sexual assault.

Wrestling coach indicted for sexual exploitation of a sixteen-year-old girl

Female teacher sentenced to three years in prison for having sex with her fourteen-year-old student.

Two students kill seventeen classmates then kill themselves. Student kills principal and wounds another.

Second-grade teacher charged with providing drugs to students.

Two students killed in gang fight at school

Three girls attack thirteen-year-old and video-tape it for Internet.

Boy carries gun to local school: shoots six.

Male teacher suspended, pending investigation of homosexual activities with male students.

Federal agents disrupt football game that allowed Jesus prayer before ball game.

Student expelled for conducting Bible classes on school campus.

Student kills principal for trying to take gun away from him.

Teacher who is teaching theory of evolution given go-ahead by school board.

Parents march to remove Bible classes from school. Drug ring busted at local school.

Local high school coach awaiting extradition for sexual assault on a sixteen-year-old girl.

Female teacher caught sending nude photos of herself to student.

After prison term completed, female teacher marries student who had fathered her child.

Gay and lesbian group ask school board to endorse homosexuality.

Boy's father files lawsuit to remove one nation under God from the Pledge of Allegiance.

School board orders principal to remove Ten Commandments displayed from his office.

Stripped of spiritualism, yoga stretches into the teachings at local school.

These are just a few samples that appear daily throughout America. These and many more recent stories in our newspapers should tell parents that it is past time for parents to take control of educating their children. If, as a parent, you try to justify that this only happens in large cities, do a little more research. These and lots of others are happening in many smaller communities. It is really clear that our school system is out of control, and there seems to be more distortion in our educational system than just taking God out. In addition, a recent survey revealed that most schools in America are ranked academically lower than most other countries.

In the past ten years, America has taken a back seat to foreign countries in producing physicians to practice in the medical field. A large majority of physicians currently practicing in America are educated in other nations. Even poor nations are turning out more doctors, educators, and professionals than rich America. In fact, it would astound most Americans if they knew how many of America's young people never finish high school. The problem must be corrected, and it seems to rest squarely on the backs of parents. It may be time to find an alternative method of schooling our young people.

PCS might be the answer.

Years past, it was the bully' that took your child's lunch money; nowadays it is the drug dealers who are taking your child's money by selling them drugs.

To Make America Stay Great Again, We Must Localize, Not Socialize, America

Many of you may not know how the title of this book came about. Actually, you may have been too young to have seen the Friday night's boxing matches on TV. Rumble was the opening line of the Friday night's fights. The first words you heard when that program came on was, "It's time to rumble." That meant the fight was starting. It was time to sit back, relax, and enjoy the fights. The title of this book, *Church! It's Time to Rumble*, is calling for the church of America to rise up and take America back. Start the fight today.

This is the last chapter of the book. And since the water from all the floods is over our heads, and we are about to drown, the only way to make America great again is to rumble. This chapter is intended to give ways to help rumble out of the mess our country is in. "I have no choice but to bring a revival to these states of the United States. Here are a few points to start the ball rolling and rerun the sting America once had back to the people.

As we have expressed several times, we are right in the middle of a civil war between the church and the states. It is a lot like the Civil War of the seventeenth century without divided sides. In the great Civil War, the South was against the North. In this war, it seems to be the Republicans against Democrats with a continuance of the holy war that has been brewing since the days of Abraham.

Before we begin to solve a problem, we must know what the problem is and then try to figure out what caused the problem. Again, I find myself turning to the Bible. Our president has called on all Americans to help him make America great again. The author of this book outlined and has published in another book that to make America great again, we must localize, not socialize, America.

To start, what the author is saying is we must move back to the initial founding of this nation. We must return to the roots that our forefathers worked so hard to establish. Here is a new ordinance we need to add to our laws: We *the people of the United States of America must once again return this nation back to the people and become a government of the people, for the people, and by the people.*

I mentioned how God usually chose one man, anointed him, and raised him up to head or lead his nation out of bondage. In the Bible, it was usually Israel who was in captivity by another country. Most of the time, Israel usually didn't even have to go to war. In fact, they usually just walked away with a victory that God gave them without fighting. Several times, God caused fear to come on the enemy to an extent that they ran away. I like what happened when Gideon lit up candles and broke a few jars, and the other armies killed each other.

Let's look at Gideon. I like to pick him as an example because I happen to be a Gideon. We are the ones who put the Bibles in the hotels and motels, hospitals, nursing homes, and others. So I like to tell about Gideon.

Remember, Gideon was the one who put the fleece out (a fleece is a lot like our sponge; it soaks up water). Gideon asked the Lord to do a test to prove that it was really God who was calling him to be the leader of his nation. You see, Gideon was the last and least in his family, and he didn't feel he was qualified to be a leader. But many times, God can't find a man that has no flaws. The first time God made the fleece wet and the ground around it dry. Next day, it was wet land and a dry fleece. This was the way God confirmed to Gideon that he was really being chosen to be the leader to deliver Israel out of bondage.

I was just thinking what President Trump has had to go through in his first term; they even impeached him. What a hard time they gave him, and even the fake newsmen caused people to hate him without a reason. Don't rule it out, he could be the one God chose to clean up and get rid of the "swamp" in congress. It keeps getting worse, and it has to be stopped.

You will have to admit that he (President Trump) had to be one of the strongest men God could have picked. Just look what he had to endure in his first term. I lost count of how many days he worked sixteen hours or more a day, didn't even draw any pay, and you would have to be blind not to see the great job he has done. If I had been on that job, I most likely would have been like Johnny Paycheck was in his song, "You can take this job and shove it."

May God bless you and your family, and may God bless America.

Selah!

PS: How many books have you seen with a PS? Many of you probably don't even know what it means. It means that I need to place a postscript. I forgot to tell you how we can bring the sting' or power back to America. It is really simple if you will do it.

The answer is found in the Bible. It tells us that there is power in the name of Jesus. The Bible even says we can cast out demons in the name of Jesus. There is power in the name of Jesus. Used to be that our forefathers used it and called on that name often. However, it seems that there are very few people in America who call on that name anymore. In fact, I made the decision to use and talk about that name in this book, knowing that some would not read the book if I did.

Church, it's time to rumble.

That's my story, and I'm sticking to it in the name of Jesus!

May God bless America and *make it great again*!

Remember, God is not dead. As I add this to the end of the book. I can tell you, I believe God has started a move to bring America back to a greatness again. And with a new leader who has vowed to "make America great again," *we'll rise again*!

ABOUT THE AUTHOR

Dal Mize is an up-and-coming writer who has authored and pub-lished three books. As a lad, Dal was taught to trust in God by his father who was an old-time circuit preacher. In this book, Dal calls on Americans to come together and rebuild the esprit de corps that our forefathers gave to us, and we need to teach it to our children.

CPSIA information can be obtained
at www.ICGtesting.com
Printed in the USA
BVHW080909240722
642332BV00002B/11

9 781684 980161